THE ILLUSTRATED HISTORY OF THE
NAZIS

THE ILLUSTRATED HISTORY OF THE
NAZIS
THE NIGHTMARE RISE AND
FALL OF ADOLF HITLER

PAUL ROLAND

CHARTWELL
BOOKS, INC.

A list of sources referenced in the text can be found on page 205.

This edition printed in 2009 by
CHARTWELL BOOKS, INC.
A Division of **BOOK SALES, INC.**
114 Northfield Avenue
Edison, New Jersey 08837

Copyright © 2009 Arcturus Publishing Limited
26/27 Bickels Yard, 151–153 Bermondsey Street,
London SE1 3HA

ISBN-13: 978-0-7858-2502-9
ISBN-10: 0-7858-2502-9
AD000250EN

Printed in China

CONTENTS

A QUESTION OF EVIL

This book differs from most conventional histories of the Third Reich in that it argues that the Nazi state was more than a sociopolitical phenomenon. Instead, it was the manifestation of its Führer's fatally flawed personality.

Sadistic criminals, serial killers and brutal dictators are routinely referred to as 'evil' and Adolf Hitler is often cited as the personification of the malevolent spirit manifest in man. But malicious spirits are a creation of the primitive, irrational mind. Common sense contends that evil is entirely man-made, that it is a deliberate, wilful act by individuals who seek satisfaction in destruction out of sheer spite and a lack of empathy for their victims.

We may not believe in the devil these days, but we continue to demonize dictators so that we are not forced to see them for what they really are – a shadow of ourselves, the embodiment of our darkest fears, a reflection of what we could become if we abandoned the conventional rules of conduct and indulged our basest instincts.

Some historians argue that Hitler was an aberration, the product of a violent, unstable era in European history that could only have come about in the aftermath of the First World War. They seek to reassure us that the milieu from which he emerged was a form of collective shell shock that is unlikely to occur again. There will always be tinpot dictators throwing their weight around, suppressing their own people and threatening their neighbours, they say, but Hitler and 'Uncle' Joe Stalin, his equally bloodthirsty ally, were the last in a line of conquerors going all the way back to Genghis Khan. These historians would have us believe that such men will be an anathema in the 21st century.

The same academics have suggested that the Nazi Party's rise to power was exclusively due to sociopolitical factors. But it is the purpose of this book to present the argument that Hitler did not wage war solely to avenge Germany's humiliating defeat in 1918. It will be shown that his insatiable appetite for conquest was not driven by territorial ambition alone nor by the desire to restore German honour and pride. Instead, the former Austrian corporal was consumed by the belief that divine Providence had entrusted him with a sacred mission, which was to subjugate all 'inferior' races and eradicate the Jews from the face of the earth.

Hitler created and nurtured a climate of suspicion, fear and deceit which pitted his own ministers against each other. He hoped that they would be too occupied with squabbling amongst themselves to plot against their Führer. But once the initial euphoria of swift and easy victory over France and the Low Countries had died down, and the reality of a protracted war with Russia filtered through, the German people woke up to the fact that they were living in a fascist police state. Anyone with a grudge could anonymously inform on a family member, friend or neighbour. They knew that their suspicions would be ruthlessly acted upon by the Gestapo, who routinely resorted to torture to extract a confession. Such conditions are not created by a unique combination of random historical events. Nazi Germany was one man's nightmare made manifest.

So if we are to understand how the Third Reich came into being – and why the German people worshipped Hitler as their saviour, even as their cities crumbled around them in the last days of 1945 – it is necessary to appreciate what kind of a mind conceived the Nazi state.

Line of conquerors: Genghis Khan, Stalin and Hitler, but what drove them to desire mastery over others?

THE MIND OF ADOLF HITLER

Hitler was a neurotic, unstable, paranoid personality whose infamous rages were a manifestation of his malignant narcissism and megalomania – which prohibited anyone from questioning his authority. Malignant narcissism is a comparatively common psychosis exhibited by violent criminals and tyrants who have a distorted view of reality and have failed to develop a sense of morality. The core components of malignant narcissism are pathological self-absorption, antisocial behaviour, a persecution complex and unconstrained aggression.

One of the characteristics of pathological narcissists is a lack of empathy for others. Unable to feel genuine emotion, they fake it by mimicking the facial expressions and language of those around them. Such people are psychologically unstable because they suffer from 'identity diffusion', which boils down to the fact that they don't have a real sense of self. Instead, they exhibit aspects of themselves as if playing a role. They have not completed the process of integration which characterizes healthy individuals – whose self-image is formed from interaction with others.

The chameleon-like character of pathological narcissists betrays the fact that they are merely acting out the role that they consider suitable to their situation. Their condition typically manifests as over-confidence and self-absorption, to a degree that makes them incapable of empathizing with others. This lack of empathy desensitizes them to such an extent that they can commit violent acts without any sense of guilt.

Malignant narcissists are devoid of conscience and are driven by self-interest. Their amorality can lead them to exploit the beliefs and convictions of others in order to consolidate their own power. They are not deterred by the threat of punishment or retribution, which makes them resistant to condemnation, censure and – in the case of tyrants – economic sanctions. Only the threat of force can deter them, because it forces them to question their belief in their own supremacy.

According to leading American political psychologist Aubrey Immelman, the malignant

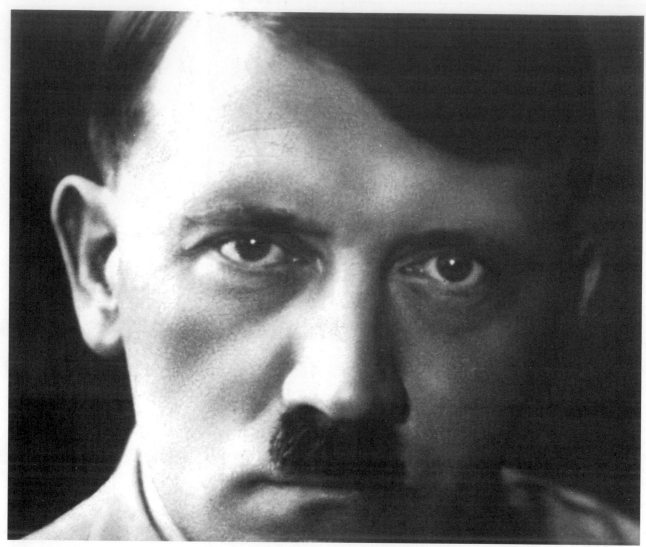

The eyes have it: few of those who met Adolf Hitler could escape his penetrating gaze

narcissist harbours a siege mentality behind his grandiose facade.

'They are insular, project their own hostilities on to others, and fail to recognize their own role in creating foes. These real or imagined enemies, in turn, are used to justify their own aggression against others. Malignant narcissists are cold, ruthless, sadistic, and cynically calculating, yet skilled at concealing their aggressive intent behind a public mask of civility or idealistic concern.'

THE 'RIGHT MAN'

Hitler was what is known in clinical psychology as a 'right man': that is, someone who stubbornly believes himself to be in the right at all times and cannot even conceive that his perspective may be distorted or that someone else may have a valid opinion. It is said that such people would 'cut off their nose to spite their face'. Such blinkered perception and stubbornness proved an asset in Hitler's early days, because his fanaticism was focused on a single objective. But such an intensely blinkered view, when allied to inflexibility, can only lead to inner conflict and ultimately to psychological disintegration and self-destruction.

Hitler could not accept defeat and when it came he ranted and raged that he would drag the nation down with him, because the German people were evidently 'unworthy' of the sacrifices he had made for them. His solution to all problems was to use threats and violence. He was devoid of conscience and had no conception of morality. 'Conscience', he said, was a Jewish invention and therefore it was the duty of the Germans to distrust it and free themselves of the 'dirty and degrading [idea of] conscience and morality'.

Even as a youth Hitler was in a state of constant denial and his grip on reality was tenuous at best.

[For a more in-depth analysis of Hitler's psychopathy see the author's *In The Minds Of Murderers – the Inside Story of Criminal Profiling*, Arcturus 2007.]

NATURE OR NURTURE?

The question of whether an individual's character is determined by nature or nurture continues to be the subject of fierce debate among psychologists, sociologists and criminologists the world over. Namely, whether evildoers act according to their nature, are compelled by some physiological impulse to seek satisfaction in antisocial acts, or whether they are conditioned to do so by their upbringing.

And while it has been proven that the brains of sociopaths and psychopaths exhibit certain physical anomalies that contribute to their aberrant behaviour, which could account for their inability to empathize with other human beings, there is no definitive study proving that criminal tendencies are the direct result of a genetic fault or some other abnormality.

However, there is compelling empirical evidence which shows that individuals who were subject to abuse in their early years are more likely to demonstrate abusive behaviour towards others when they reach their teens and adulthood. Moreover, they will commit those

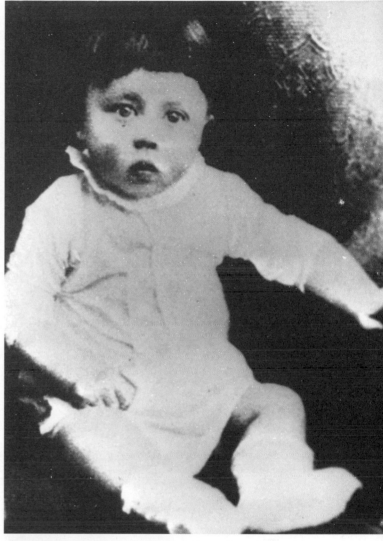

Adolf Hitler at about a year old: did he lose his innocence or was he born bad?

acts knowing that they are wrong and in spite of the consequences.

Whether Adolf Hitler suffered an abusive childhood to the extent that his many biographers have described, or whether he was simply a product of the turbulent times in which he lived, is debatable. However, he evidently lacked the strength of character to come to terms with his early experiences and the temperament to exorcise, or at least subdue, his personal demons. He appears to have been bedevilled by his upbringing and his own perverse nature, which saw him nurture his resentments until they consumed him – but not before he had taken his rage out on the world.

CHAPTER ONE
HITLER'S EARLY LIFE

BAD BLOOD

Of the many odd twists of fate that affected the life of the future Führer, perhaps none is more significant than that which occurred 13 years before his birth. His paternal grandfather belatedly legitimized his own 39-year-old bastard son Alois (Adolf's father) by changing his name from Schicklgruber to Hitler in order that Alois could share in an inheritance bequeathed by an uncle. Had he not done so it is conceivable that Hitler might never have come to prominence, for there is power in a name and it is hard to imagine the German people venerating Adolf Schicklgruber as they did Adolf Hitler. ('Heil Schicklgruber' does not have quite the same impact!)

Various authors have speculated that the name change was effected for a more sinister reason. That is, in order to silence persistent local rumours that Alois' real father was a Graz Jew named Frankenberger who had employed Adolf's grandmother, Maria Anna Schicklgruber, as a domestic servant. This might explain why Hitler ordered four secret investigations into his ancestry between 1932 and 1940 and why the findings were never disclosed. It would also account for his otherwise inexplicable destruction of his father's birthplace, Dollersheim, and the levelling of the graveyard in which his grandmother was buried, as well as the burning of the parish records. It has even been argued that Hitler grew his Chaplinesque moustache to disguise what he believed was his characteristically Semitic nose and that he subjected himself to periodic purging by leeches, and later by hypodermic needle, to 'cleanse' himself of his 'contaminated' blood.

Whatever the truth of these rumours, Adolf's forebears on his father's side were clearly not the sturdy stock that would produce the future Master Race. They were itinerant farm labourers and work-shy peasants whose habitual intermarriage produced an uncommonly high number of physically disabled or imbecile children. Secret Gestapo files now stored in the US Library of Congress and in the Institut für Zeitgeschichte Archiv in Munich record several stunted branches on the family tree including that of Joseph Veit, a cousin of Hitler's father who bore three mentally retarded children, one of whom was to commit suicide in a mental institution. According to an affidavit signed by Dr Edward Kriechbaum and stored in the Linz archives, Adolf's aunt Johanna was said to be schizophrenic, while his cousin Edward Schmidt was a hunchback who also suffered from a speech impediment.

The family practitioner Dr Bloch testified to the OSS (Office of Strategic Services) in 1936 that Hitler had a sister whom he suspected was mentally retarded because she was always hidden away whenever he visited her parent's home. He also said that Adolf's younger sister, Paula, was a 'high grade moron'. The inbreeding which appears to have been characteristic of the Hitler line could account for his infamous rages. It would also explain his fear of inherent insanity, his repugnance for physical deformity

'THESE PEOPLE [JOURNALISTS] MUST NEVER FIND OUT WHO I AM. THEY MUSTN'T KNOW WHERE I COME FROM OR MY FAMILY BACKGROUND.'
Adolf Hitler[1]

Driven man: did Hitler's turbulent nature compel him to forge a new order?

and his belief that if he married he risked producing 'feeble-minded' children.

By comparison, Hitler's maternal ancestry was slightly more stable. His mother's family had been smallholders in the village of Spital in Lower Austria, near Vienna for four generations, but were considered by the inhabitants of the capital to be no better than peasants. They were despised as much for their ignorance as for their lowly origins and their humourless, suspicious nature.

HITLER'S MOTHER

Klara Pölzl, Hitler's adored mother, was a simple, fastidiously neat young woman with a somewhat boyish face and piercing blue eyes. They were a feature that her only surviving son was to inherit and with which he would later enthrall his admirers. Klara had little expectation of improving her situation until, at the age of 16, she moved in with her 'Uncle' Alois and his first wife Anna Glassl as their unpaid domestic servant. Alois apparently wasted little time in pursuing both Klara and the maid Franziska Matzelberger until Anna got wise and insisted on a separation. Alois then set up home with Franziska (or 'Fanni' as she was called) who demanded that her rival be packed off to Vienna. Alois and Franziska married three years later when he was 46 years old and she was just 22. The couple had two children – a son, Alois jnr., and a daughter, Angela – before Franziska succumbed to a fatal bout of tuberculosis, prompting her husband to summon Klara back from the city to look after the children.

Alois Matzelberger (who later took the surname Hitler) grew up to become an embarrassment to his famous half-brother. He was twice convicted of theft and once jailed for bigamy. After a brief spell in Britain he deserted his family and returned to Berlin where he ran a beer keller and stubbornly refused to discuss his family history for fear of angering Adolf. Angela, Adolf Hitler's half-sister, fared better. She married well and after her husband's death went to live with Adolf in Berchtesgaden as his cook and housekeeper. But when she left him in 1936 to remarry, Hitler exhibited his infamous vindictiveness and refused to send her a wedding present.

Klara appears to have harboured no ill feeling towards Anna for she nursed her during her final illness. However, while Franziska lay dying, her philandering husband pressed his attentions upon his adopted 'niece' and succeeded in getting her pregnant. He then attempted to 'put things right' by marrying her when her condition aroused the attention of the village gossips.

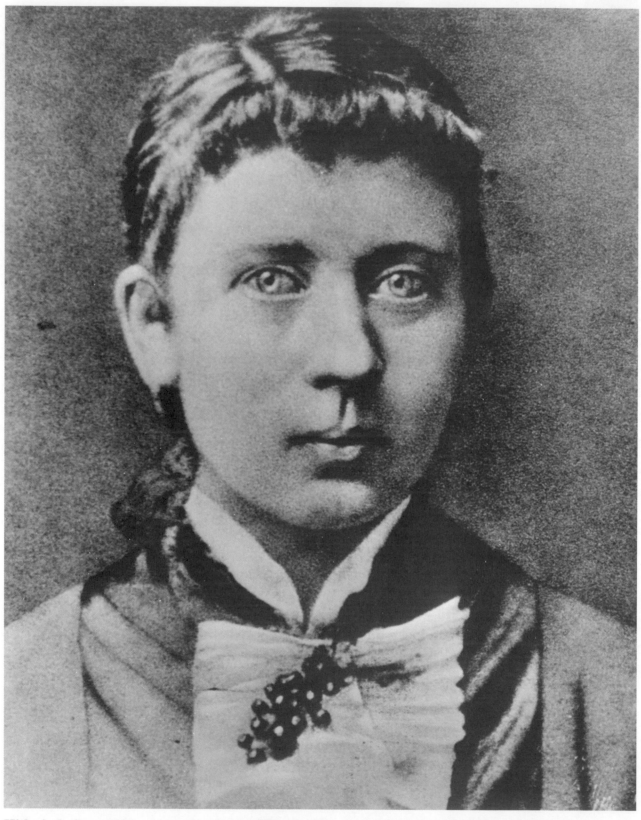

Hitler's doting mother was a simple, fastidiously neat young woman with piercing blue eyes

Because Klara was Alois' second cousin, the couple had to apply for an episcopal dispensation in order to marry. The wedding took place at the parish church of Braunau in January 1885, at six o'clock on an overcast winter's morning. Klara was then 25 years old and four months pregnant and her twice-widowed husband was 48. Four months later their first child, Gustav, was born, followed by a daughter Ida in 1886.

Adolf was their third child and their only surviving son because the two older siblings died in infancy and a third, Adolf's younger brother Edmund (b.1894), was to die at the age of six. Only Adolf and a younger sister, Paula (b.1896), survived.

Klara was a devout Catholic and must have been wracked with guilt at having deceived Alois' former wives. She considered herself to have sinned against them and survived and her guilt must have been compounded by the death of her first two children from diphtheria the year before Adolf was born. It is likely that she might have seen their painful and protracted deaths as divine punishment. For the same reason she might have borne her husband's alleged beatings without protest, as penance for her imagined sins.

MOTHER LOVE

Adolf Hitler was born at half past six in the evening of April 20, 1889 in the village of Braunau am Inn in Austria, within sight of the Bavarian mountains. Hitler considered the location to be highly significant and later wrote that he believed that fate had chosen Braunau as his birthplace so that he would make it his life's mission to reunite the German-speaking peoples on both sides of the border.

Adolf was by all accounts a sickly, demanding child whose condition must have increased his mother's innate anxiety while helping to assuage her guilt. If he survived she could see it as proof that her penance had been paid and so she doted on him to the detriment of the boy's emotional and psychological development. Her compulsive cleaning of their home and her obsessive attention to the cleanliness of her children were further indications of her need to scrub the shame and guilt away. Hitler's own fastidiousness and his obsession with personal hygiene in adulthood were perhaps the direct results of his mother's neurosis. It also led to his unnatural obsession with bodily functions and his belief that germs were targeting him specifically. But for all his mother's mollycoddling she could not protect him from repeated beatings at the hand of her husband. Her failure to intervene rankled with her son, who must have resented her weakness as much as he cursed his father's cruelty. Dr Bloch, the family doctor, described the relationship between mother and son as uncommonly close, while acknowledging that their neighbours thought it was unnatural.

Adolf grew up hating his father and revering his mother, creating in his mind a syndrome known as primitive idealization whereby a child imagines that one parent is wholly virtuous and the other is entirely bad. Many children who are conditioned in this way adjust their distorted perspective when they realize that the ideal parent has failings too and that the other parent has redeeming qualities. But Hitler's childhood world of absolutes remained with him to the end and gave him a false sense of security. His worldview was distorted through the mirror of his own warped ego and he would not be reasoned with. That is why he flew into a rage whenever his authority was questioned.

A BRUTAL UPBRINGING?

Adolf Hitler was a compulsive fantasist whose penchant for myth-making obscured the truth of his early life. He cast himself as the victim of an abusive, alcoholic father who routinely beat his son and prevented him from pursuing his dream of becoming an artist.

According to those who knew him, Alois was a strict, domineering, officious, hot-tempered and humourless man who ruled his household with a rod of iron. He insisted that he be obeyed without question and that his children address him formally as 'Herr Vater'. They were not to speak until given permission to do so and Adolf was often summoned with a whistle, like a dog, rather than being called by name. It must have demeaned the boy to have had the pet Alsatian named after him and to have been treated no better than the animal. The only extant photo of the father portrays a portly and proud provincial official. In his Austrian customs service uniform, with his close-cropped hair and bushy handlebar moustache, he looked every inch the old Prussian aristocrat he must have dreamt of being.

As a child Adolf elicited sympathy from other children by claiming to have dragged his drunken father from the village inn on many occasions. Later in his life he recalled: 'That was the most shameful, humiliating experience I have ever had. How well I know what a devil alcohol is. It was – because of my father – the greatest enemy of my youth!' [3]

'NO PERSON MANIFESTING HITLER'S PATHOLOGICAL PERSONALITY TRAITS COULD POSSIBLY HAVE GROWN UP IN THE IDYLLIC HOME ENVIRONMENT HITLER HIMSELF HAS DESCRIBED.'
Walter Langer [2]

But Alois was not an alcoholic. In fact, he was much respected in the customs service, in which he had attained a high rank. His position had given him sufficient income to buy a pleasant house in the village of Fischlham near Linz, which boasted nine acres of land, fruit trees and a splendid view of the surrounding countryside. His wages were on a par with that of a country lawyer and even after his retirement in 1895, when Adolf was six years old, he benefited from a generous pension of 2,660 kronen, on which the family could live very comfortably. So the picture of an impoverished, abusive childhood is all a myth of Hitler's own making, although it is true that his childhood was unsettled in so far as the family moved repeatedly for no apparent reason.

By the time Adolf was 15 years old he had attended five different schools and could recall seven different homes, including a renovated mill and a period when the family were guests at a local inn. After that they finally settled in the village of Leonding, where they purchased a modest furnished apartment, by which time the volatile relationship between father and son had become a battle of wills. The old man, now in his 60s, insisted that his son follow him into the civil service while Adolf stubbornly refused to study in the hope of forcing his father to allow him to follow his ambition to become a painter.

'No matter how firm and determined my father might be, his son was just as stubborn and obstinate,' Hitler wrote in *Mein Kampf*.

Alois Schicklgruber was a strict and domineering father who ruled his household with a rod of iron

A rare photo of the young Hitler, aged 10, at school in Lambach: he was not an outstanding pupil

It is clear from his remarks in later life that he both respected and feared his father, but he was determined to distance himself from the old man by his actions. Adolf's aversion to tobacco stemmed from memories of his father's habit of smoking in the house from morning to night, while his mother invoked his father's unimpeachable authority by pointing to the row of pipes on the kitchen shelves. Hitler also grew to detest his father's obsession with punctuality, which he sneered at in later life by lying in bed until lunchtime – to the frustration of his ministers and visiting dignitaries. Even Alois' rule forbidding idle talk was to influence his son's behaviour because Adolf often indulged in rambling reminiscences with his guests (the so-called 'table talks') and aimless all-night monologues with his long-suffering valet. But ultimately he could not help becoming that which he had detested. Like his father before him, Hitler was humourless and hot-tempered and he would not tolerate his orders being questioned or his opinions contradicted.

CHILDHOOD TRAUMA

The arrival of Adolf's brother Edmund in 1894, when Adolf was six, prompted Klara to entrust him to his then married half-sister Angela, thus robbing him of his mother's undivided attention at a critical age. It is said that he prayed for God to take the infant as he had his deceased brother and sister. Although it was to be six years before Edmund died of complications following a bout of measles, the belated fulfilment of this childish curse would have left an indelible psychic scar on the surviving sibling. Edmund's premature death is likely to have reinforced Adolf's conviction that he alone had been spared because he was special. His mother had made this assertion so often that it had imprinted itself on his mind, to the extent that he could not fail to believe that he was protected by Providence, singled out to fulfil some special mission.

Despite the fact that Edmund's death was what Adolf had wanted, he would have suffered from extreme guilt if he had believed that the event had brought grief upon his mother. And his feelings would have been compounded by the manner in which Edmund was laid to rest. His parents flatly refused to attend their son's funeral and instead spent the day in Linz as if nothing untoward had occurred, leaving 11-year-old Adolf to grieve alone. It is thought that Alois had forbidden his wife to attend the funeral merely because he had fallen out with the local priest. Alois is known to have argued with the priest over 'political' differences and Klara was too submissive to defy him – even to the extent of missing her own son's funeral. One can only wonder at Adolf Hitler's state of mind as he stood watching his brother's body being lowered into the frozen ground while a biting blizzard whipped about the grave.

However, it was not long before Adolf witnessed an event that must have seemed like divine retribution for his father's uncharitable act. On the morning of 23 January 1903 Alois Hitler died from a massive haemorrhage while taking his daily beaker of wine at the local inn. He was 66. Adolf did not mourn his passing.

SCHOOL LIFE

The period immediately following his father's death was one of liberation for the sullen adolescent, who was finally free of the suffocating shadow of the overbearing old man. And yet his new-found freedom did not produce an improvement in his school work. Hitler later claimed that his poor grades were due to the fact that he had deliberately neglected his studies in the hope that his father would relent and allow him to pursue his ambition to become an artist. But after his father's death his report cards continued to record a steady decline when he could so easily have applied himself, if only to make his mother proud. Instead, his increasing arrogance, lack of attentiveness and poor marks prompted his expulsion from the Realschule in Linz at the age of 15, forcing his widowed mother to send him to the state high school in Styr 15 miles (24 kilometres) away, where he was to continue his education.

Although Hitler later claimed that Klara was destitute at this time, in fact she was far from it. She received a widow's pension which was roughly two-thirds of her late husband's income, plus a generous lump sum of 650 kronen from his former employer. With the sale of the family home in June 1905 she was able to pay for Adolf's lodgings in Styr and move into a spacious apartment in the Humboldtstrasse in Linz, in order to be near her married step-daughter Angela.

Hitler's academic failure could be attributed to a normal adolescent aversion to authority and an unwillingness to work at subjects in which he had little interest. He might also have hoped that the generous widow's pension his mother received would make it possible for him to pursue the bohemian lifestyle he had long

dreamt of. If so, her insistence that he should continue to attend school must have seemed like an act of betrayal, but he would have vented his frustration on his teachers rather than his doting mother. That would explain his lifelong distrust of academics and experts of all kinds. To the end of his life he was intimidated by intellectuals and chose to surround himself with sycophants and shallow, servile admirers who would reassure him of his genius.

With the exception of his history teacher at Linz, who described Hitler's grasp of the subject as no more than 'fair', and a science master who admitted that his former pupil was unremarkable, he was disparaging of his masters, seeing them as his 'natural enemies'. He described them as 'erudite apes', 'slightly mad', 'effete', 'abnormal' and 'mentally deranged' – which probably reveals more about Hitler's state of mind than it does about the academic abilities of his teachers.

For a more reliable impression of the future Führer as a youth there is Professor Huemer's testimony from Hitler's trial following the abortive Beer Hall Putsch in Munich in 1923. Huemer conceded that Hitler was 'gifted' in certain subjects but recalled that: '... he lacked self-control and, to say the least, he was considered argumentative, autocratic, self-opinionated and bad-tempered and unable to submit to school discipline. Nor was he industrious, otherwise he would have achieved much better results, gifted as he was.'

> HE WAS CONSIDERED ARGUMENTATIVE, AUTOCRATIC, SELF-OPINIONATED AND BAD-TEMPERED AND UNABLE TO SUBMIT TO SCHOOL DISCIPLINE.

Hitler surrounded himself with sycophants who succumbed meekly to his domineering will

PHYSICAL ABNORMALITY

There is another explanation for Hitler's poor academic achievements which merits consideration, even though it may appear inconsequential to the lay person. It has been suggested that Hitler was a monorchid: that is, that he only had one testicle, a condition which produces a number of characteristic behavioural disorders. These are the very aberrations that Adolf Hitler exhibited. He had learning difficulties; a lack of concentration; the compulsion to fantasize and lie; social and sexual inadequacy; an attraction to physical danger; an aversion to criticism; and a feeling of being in some way 'special' (this is presumably a defence mechanism to explain the 'abnormality').

Hitler's monorchidism was discovered during a Soviet autopsy on the Führer's charred remains, which was conducted in 1945. Although the identity of the body found in the grounds of the Reichschancellery has been disputed, an independent team of Norwegian and American dental experts has now confirmed that it was Hitler's corpse.[4]

A monorchid child does not automatically exhibit such neuroses and can be expected to overcome the fear that his condition makes him somehow less of a man, but if a boy is already psychologically disturbed this uncommon condition can intensify his psychosis. Such symptoms typically manifest themselves in pre-pubescence, the period in which Hitler's academic achievements went into decline.

'MY ARM IS LIKE GRANITE – RIGID AND UNBENDING... IT'S AN AMAZING FEAT. I MARVEL AT MY OWN POWER.'
Adolf Hitler

An early sketch by a classmate depicts the 15-year-old Adolf as an unimposing youth, but one who would presumably have had as much luck with the local girls as any of his contemporaries. The fact that Hitler avoided romantic entanglements of any kind, preferring to fantasize about girls he never had the courage to talk to, suggests something more than the usual adolescent awkwardness. He could have experienced a fear of intimacy that may have had a physical and a psychological basis.

It would not be unreasonable to imagine that Hitler, in his ignorance, would blame his mother for his condition. Her repeated assurances that all would be well were to prove unfounded and this would have served to intensify his anxiety, adding to his catalogue of violently conflicting emotions.

CASTRATION COMPLEX

It is not uncommon for monorchid boys to develop a castration complex. The more disturbed children among them might even compensate for this feeling by indulging in violent fantasies involving the emasculation of their enemies. It is significant that in adulthood Hitler repeatedly talked of castrating those artists who displeased him and that he reintroduced beheading as a form of execution when a firing squad would have sufficed.

It has been noted that boys who are missing a testicle, or whose testicles have not descended, often exhibit their anxiety concerning their sexual identity by clutching their genitals for

Hitler was frequently seen with his hands clasped together in a defensive gesture

reassurance or by putting a hand over their crotch. It cannot be coincidence that this is precisely the gesture that Hitler can be seen making repeatedly in newsreel footage, in countless photographs and even in official portraits. Whatever the situation, he is frequently seen with his hands folded over his crotch in a protective gesture. His hands are only fleetingly placed behind his back and they are rarely visible at his sides.

Hitler was also known to indulge in infantile displays of what he believed were masculine feats of strength and endurance – but they were clearly sexual substitutes. On one occasion he attempted to impress a female guest at his mountain retreat in the Obersalzberg by keeping his arm in the Nazi salute position for a long period of time. After assuring her that he could keep it up longer than Goering, he said, 'I can hold my arm like that for two solid hours. My arm is like granite – rigid and unbending... It's an amazing feat. I marvel at my own power.'[5]

It has been noted that monorchid men invariably transfer their sexual energy to their eyes. Hitler is said to have practised and perfected his penetrating stare in the mirror, no doubt as a substitute for sexual gratification.

As unlikely as it might sound to those not steeped in Freudian psychology, it would certainly explain Hitler's infamous and otherwise inexplicable hypnotic power. It will be remembered that many of those who found themselves in Hitler's presence commented on the hypnotic quality of his piercing blue, greenish-grey eyes.

A boyhood friend, August Kubizek, recalled in his biography *The Young Hitler I Knew* (Boston 1955) that his mother was frightened by Hitler's penetrating gaze.

'I remember quite distinctly that there was more fear than admiration in her words... Adolf spoke with his eyes... Never in my life have I seen any other person whose appearance... was so completely dominated by the eyes.'

When Hitler ranted against those who failed to recognize his genius, his friend remembers that his face was livid and his lips were clenched white with fury.

'But the eyes glittered. There was something sinister about them. As if all the hate of which he was capable lay in those glowing eyes.'

Even at the very end, as he shuffled through the Berlin bunker in April 1945, a shell of his former self, his eyes retained their power. A young adjutant recalled that even in the last hours of his life they were 'strangely penetrating'.

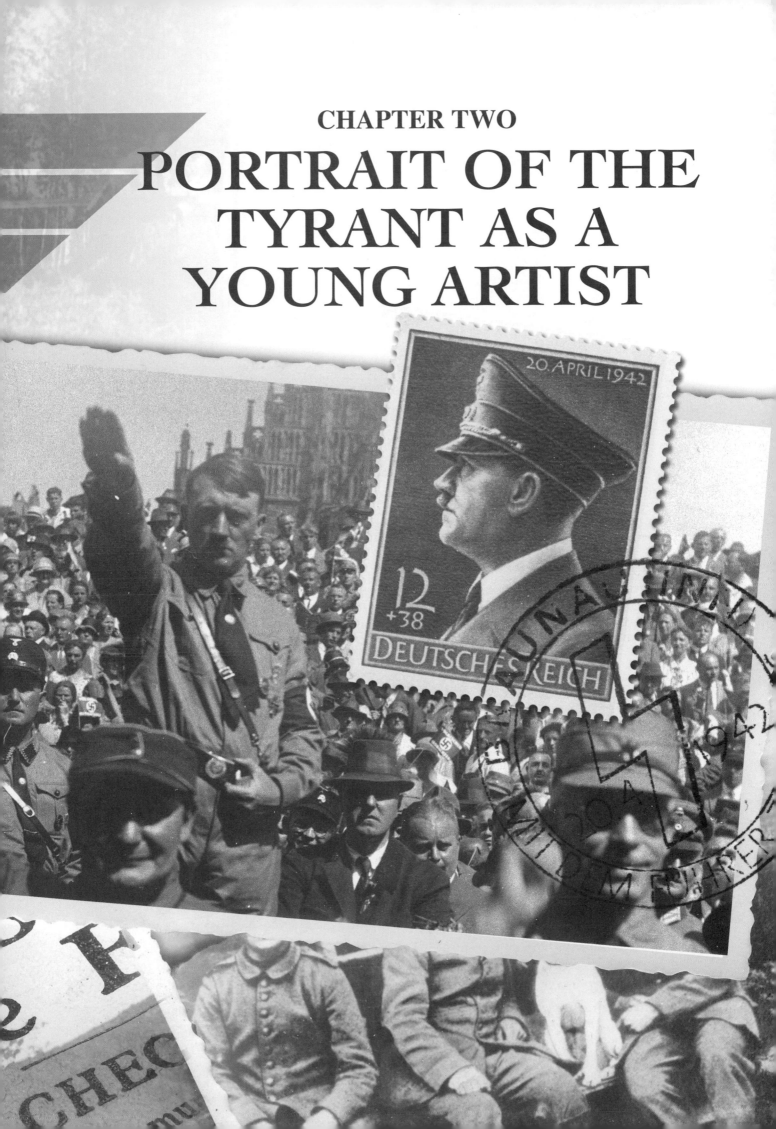

CHAPTER TWO
PORTRAIT OF THE TYRANT AS A YOUNG ARTIST

ADOLF IN CRISIS

Hitler's frustration at not being allowed to pursue his artistic ambitions came to a head when he succumbed to what he later claimed was a serious lung infection (quite possibly a psychosomatic disorder) in his final year at Styr. He appealed to his mother to allow him to return home to convalesce and to his relief she relented. She was not in the best of health at the time, so she insisted that he stay with his aunt Theresa in Spital. Curiously, the family doctor, Dr Bloch, dismissed the entire episode as a figment of Hitler's fevered imagination and implied that he was simply malingering to elicit his mother's sympathy.

As he recalled, 'I cannot understand the many references to his lung trouble as a youth. I was the only doctor treating him during the period... My records show nothing of the sort... There was never anything seriously wrong with Hitler.' [6]

After making a miraculous recovery he persuaded his mother to purchase a piano so that he could write his own operas, but he quickly tired of his teacher, who demanded that he practise his scales rather than rely on his natural genius. Undaunted he threw himself into what he later called the 'hollowness of a comfortable life'. He indulged his passion for attending the opera, museums and art galleries in Linz and he dressed in style – all, of course, at his mother's expense.

In his black silk-lined overcoat, tweed jacket, cravat and kid gloves Hitler was every inch the young man about town, but no matter how hard he affected the air of a gentleman he must have known he was only playing the part. August Kubizek, the only close acquaintance of his youth, was his companion on his almost nightly expeditions to the city during those carefree years. Although it was clear that he was the truly talented one, Kubizek patiently endured Adolf's rambling sermons on the merits of true German art. He also tolerated his embittered political rants against the decadent Hapsburg monarchy, which was fast becoming an obsession.

Kubizek recalled, 'He saw everywhere only obstacles and hostility. He was always up against something and at odds with the world... I never saw him take anything lightly.'

> 'HE SAW EVERYWHERE ONLY OBSTACLES AND HOSTILITY. HE WAS ALWAYS UP AGAINST SOMETHING AND AT ODDS WITH THE WORLD... I NEVER SAW HIM TAKE ANYTHING LIGHTLY.'

DESTINY CALLING

In the early hours of a chill November morning in 1906 Hitler and Kubizek emerged from the opera house in Linz with the last strains of Wagner's *Rienzi* still ringing in their ears.

For Kubizek, the music student, the evening was to prove a memorable one and not because of the performance they had just enjoyed. That night he was treated to a performance of an entirely different nature, quite possibly the first evidence of Hitler's gift for oratory, when he delivered an impassioned speech under the stars on the deserted road leading up the Freinberg.

Hitler's earlier monologues, witnessed at a distance by his Realschule professor and other children, had been addressed to the trees on a hill in Leonding, but this night was different. He

'Ein Volk, Ein Reich, Ein Führer': Hitler's indomitable will ensured that the fantasy he first outlined to August Kubizek in 1906 became a fearful reality – as seen here at Nuremberg in 1928

The new Messiah: Hitler instilled a quasi-religious fanaticism through his powers of oratory

had grown tired of imagining and now demanded a real audience. Wheeling around, he took his startled friend by the hands and stared fixedly into his eyes as if willing the boy to submit. Kubizek could not remember what was said that morning, but he would never forget the intensity with which the 17-year-old Hitler poured forth his diatribe against society and his determination to dedicate his life to saving the German people.

'It was as if another being spoke out of his body and moved him as much as it did me. It was not at all a case of a speaker carried away by his own words. On the contrary; I rather felt as though he himself listened with astonishment and emotion to what burst forth from him with elemental force… like floodwaters breaking their dykes, his words burst from him. He conjured up in grandiose inspiring pictures his own future and that of his people. He was talking of a Mandate which, one day, he would receive from the people to lead them from servitude to the heights of freedom – a special mission which would one day be entrusted to him.'

POWER OVER THE MASSES

Clearly Hitler had a sense of his own destiny, but it was one in which Kubizek was to play no part. That night he realized that Hitler only sought his company because he needed an audience.

'I came to understand that our friendship endured largely for the reason that I was a patient listener… He just HAD TO TALK…'

The compulsion to talk appears to have come from Hitler's need to dominate others with the power of his voice and the force of his argument. In time, it has been said, his speeches would take on a decidedly sexual quality.

He would begin in a low, seductive tone and build up to an ecstatic climax after which he would retire from the podium drained of strength and drenched in sweat, with a glazed look of satisfaction in his eyes.

The Polish journalist Axel Heyst witnessed Hitler's power over the masses, but remained unmoved. 'In his speeches we hear the suppressed voice of passion and wooing, which is taken from the language of love. He utters a cry of hate and voluptuousness, a spasm of violence and cruelty. All those tones and sounds are taken from the back streets of the instincts; they remind us of dark impulses repressed too long.'

The poet René Schickele was more direct. He damned Hitler's speeches as oral 'rape and murder'.

The intimate nature of the relationship between orator and audience was not lost on the Führer himself who said, 'One must know exactly when the moment has come to throw the last flaming javelin which sets the crowd afire.'

For such people verbal intercourse is often a substitute for sexual relations, which they avoid for fear of ridicule. Oral discharge, as the psychoanalysts would term it, keeps the object of desire at a distance. There may be some truth in this Freudian analysis of Hitler's powers of oratory, but those who have seen newsreel footage of the Führer in full flight have often gained the impression that Hitler was merely a man who was seduced by the sound of his own voice.

UNREQUITED LOVE

Hitler's oratory was clearly powered by an unbridled animal passion and for that reason they had an extraordinary effect on a live audience. At the same time, they made no lasting impression when seen in print or on film, unlike the speeches of Winston Churchill, for example, whose eloquent words appealed to the intellect.

It is arguable that Hitler might have channelled his energy into less destructive ends if he had allowed himself to indulge in an intimate relationship in his youth. But he was incapable of relating to other people. Aside from his innate distrust and paranoia he also manifested symptoms of a form of erotomania, the belief that he

Under the influence: Hitler envisaged his first love as a pure Wagnerian heroine

was involved in a romantic relationship which did not exist.

In the winter of 1906 Hitler came across a girl named Stefanie. She was window shopping in the Landstrasse in Linz with her mother and he became infatuated with her. Typically, he preferred to worship her from afar, so every afternoon at precisely 5 o'clock he waited where he had first seen her, hoping for a fleeting glimpse of his beloved. Every gesture would be analyzed in the hope of finding a sign of approval. His only concession to convention was to write reams of absurdly romantic poetry in which he envisaged her as a pure Wagnerian heroine, none of which he thought to send her. He could not summon up the courage to speak to her and so was able to avoid the risk of rejection. So long as he didn't approach her he could continue his fantasy, for what if this symbol of Germanic virtue spurned him? The prospect was too hideous to contemplate.

After months of martyrdom he wrote her an earnest, anonymous letter. He began by declaring his love and ended by begging her to wait four years until he had made his name and could marry her. Until then he would make what he considered to be the supreme gesture. He would leave home to live the life of an impoverished artist in Vienna. But there may have been more mundane reasons for his departure. Relatives were asking uncomfortable questions – when was he going to earn his own living and not be entirely dependent on his mother?

VIENNA

And so it was that in the spring of 1906, just after his 17th birthday, Hitler turned his back on Linz and set out for Vienna, the bustling cosmopolitan capital of culture and the jewel in the crown of the old Hapsburg Empire. As he strolled through the historic centre gazing up at the imposing imperial symbols of power he visualized himself presenting the treasures of the Reich in a new setting with himself as its chief architect.

In Hitler's deluded mind the years he spent in Vienna were a time of martyrdom, of intolerable suffering in body and soul. He imagined himself being forced to take a succession of manual labouring jobs, like shovelling snow or breaking his back on building sites. In fact, he didn't do an honest day's work during that period, but lived very comfortably on the generosity of his relatives. The only exception was a 15-month period from September 1908 to December 1909 when he depended on the charity of Jewish welfare organizations, a helping hand he must have accepted begrudgingly to say the least. Only when he found himself needing extra money did he paint a few postcards of the sites. They were bought mainly by Jewish gallery owners who were later forced to return them when the Nazis sought to erase the Führer's past.

DISILLUSIONMENT

It was not until a year later, in October 1907, that Hitler's illusions of imminent fame and fortune finally came crashing to the ground.

That autumn he was rejected by the Vienna Academy of Fine Arts, whose examining board considered his drawings 'unsatisfactory'.

Determined to prove the academy's experts wrong he persuaded his crippled aunt Johanna to become a patron of the arts by supporting his ambitions from her life savings. Her contributions were supplemented by an orphan's pension of 25 kronen per month, obtained by deception from the state. The money should have been paid to his sister Paula, but Hitler had made a false declaration stating that he was a student at the Academy, which entitled him to her share. A court order corrected the situation in May 1911.

Added to that sum he received a small inheritance from a great aunt, Walpurga Hitler, and on his 18th birthday, April 1907, he became legally entitled to his share of his father's savings which had been accumulating interest for over three years and now amounted to 700 kronen. In total he received the equivalent of a school teacher's salary during those aimless years in Vienna and did not put in a day's work to earn it. Instead he spent the afternoons in idle daydreaming. He planned new buildings for the capital that, he assured the doggedly loyal Kubizek, he would be commissioned to build once the city fathers recognized his genius. When he tired of sketching he made plans for a Reich Orchestra which would tour the country bringing German culture to the masses. He would personally select the programme from works he judged to be suitable. That is, music he had heard while accompanying his friend to concerts on an almost nightly basis, thanks to the allocation of free tickets from the Conservatory, where Kubizek was then studying composition.

While Kubizek pursued his studies he and Hitler were amiable companions, though it was evident that Hitler considered his friend his inferior. They even shared a room together for a time in the Sixth District, which was large enough to house Kubizek's grand piano. But after Kubizek graduated with honours from the Vienna Conservatory Hitler felt increasingly uncomfortable. Kubizek's presence reminded Hitler of his own unfulfilled ambitions. From that moment on, he and Kubizek were barely on speaking terms.

THE DEATH OF HITLER'S MOTHER

In December 1907, Hitler's life of idleness was interrupted by the death of his mother. Klara had been diagnosed with cancer of the breast and had been hospitalized in January of that year. A mastectomy was performed by the house surgeon, assisted by Dr Bloch, who continued to care for her after she returned home. She recovered well enough to take short walks through the village that summer, but in November she suffered a relapse and Dr Bloch had to administer large doses of morphine to ease the pain. Dr Bloch, Hitler's sister Paula, August Kubizek and the local postmistress have all testified that Adolf hurried home from Vienna to be at his mother's bedside. But their stories of the dutiful son scrubbing floors and attending to her every need are contradicted by Franz Jetzinger in his biography *Hitler's Youth*. Jetzinger quotes a neighbour who claimed to have tended Klara in those final weeks. Her version of events sounds more plausible because she shared her recollection of Klara's last days with others at the time and she was able to produce a letter written by Hitler thanking her for having tended his mother in his absence. Her story also appears to be substantiated by the fact that when she herself was ill her hospital care was paid for by a grateful Führer.

It has been suggested by some that Hitler's anti-Semitism began when he blamed the Jewish family physician for not saving his mother, or for prolonging her agony by administering the wrong treatment. Others say that if Hitler had been too preoccupied with his own pleasure to attend his dying mother, or had deliberately stayed away because he could not see her suffer, he would have bitterly resented Dr Bloch for assuming the role of dutiful carer – a role that was rightfully his.

But this is not supported by the evidence. Dr Bloch received several hand-painted postcards at the time of Klara's death, in which Hitler expressed his profuse gratitude for the compassion and care with which his mother's passing had been eased. Also, the physician continued to speak of Hitler as a doting son after he had emigrated to America and was safe from the attentions of the Gestapo.

Perhaps the most intriguing question, and one which will doubtless remain unanswered, is why Hitler refused to mark his mother's grave with a headstone. It was only after he became Chancellor of Germany that local Nazi Party activists noted the omission and erected a gravestone at their own expense. When Hitler visited the cemetery in 1938 for the first and last time he stood for only a few seconds and then turned and walked briskly back to his waiting car. If he loved his mother as much as he professed to do and the affection had been mutual, why did he deny her a memorial? What dark and disturbing secret had died with her?

CHAPTER THREE
INSIDIOUS INFLUENCES

ORIGINS OF HITLER'S ANTI-SEMITISM

It is arguable that Hitler's ambivalent feelings towards Dr Bloch sowed the seeds of the virulent anti-Semitism that surfaced just months later. His feelings towards the Jewish physician must have been a mixture of gratitude and resentment, for the doctor possessed the compassion and the medical knowledge to be a comfort to his mother when he could only stand helplessly by, if indeed he was there at all. A neurotic, morose, self-centred person like Hitler would have been eaten up by such conflicting emotions, unless he could have found a substitute to blame for all his troubles. Unable to confront Dr Bloch with his true feelings he would in all likelihood have turned on the Jews in general. As a good Catholic he could not reproach God for his loss. Instead he would have internalized his anguish and when it threatened to consume him he would have spewed it out like an overflowing volcano. The Jews were a target that he had cynically sized up in the knowledge that they would not fight back.

Jew baiting was widespread in Europe at the time and the pernicious influence of the Jews would have been an accepted topic of conversation at all levels of Austrian society. Several anti-Semitic societies and periodicals openly promoted the disenfranchising of the Jews and spread vicious lies regarding Jewish religious rites, which were said to involve the sacrifice of Christian children. Even 'respectable' politicians felt safe in voicing their irrational prejudices in a public forum. In a speech to the Vienna parliament in 1887, Georg Schonerer sought to justify his views.

'Our anti-Semitism is not directed against the Jews' religion. It is directed against their racial characteristics… everywhere they are in league with the forces of rebellion… Therefore every loyal son of his nation must see in anti-Semitism the greatest national progress of this century.'

In Hitler's case it would appear that he also had the Jews to blame for his rejection at the Academy of Art in Vienna. This happened on two separate occasions, for he reapplied in October 1908 and was rejected out of hand. On the second attempt the board took a cursory glance at his sample sketches and refused to allow him to take the entrance test. He still nurtured the hope that he might be allowed to apply for a place at the School of Architecture, but that faded with the realization that he couldn't fulfil the minimum requirements for entry because he hadn't completed his formal education. It must have been a shattering blow to his inflated ego when he discovered that all his plans were to be frustrated by petty officials. He was perhaps reminded of his father's earlier objections to his artistic ambitions. Unable to accept the fact that he lacked the abilities he thought he possessed, he blamed the Academy for being blind to his genius.

He admitted many years later that he had investigated the racial origins of the admissions

> 'THE DRAGON OF INTERNATIONAL JEWRY MUST BE SLAUGHTERED SO THAT OUR DEAR GERMAN PEOPLE CAN BE FREED FROM THEIR PRISON.'
> *Dr Karl Lueger (1844–1910), Mayor of Vienna*

Jew baiting was widespread in Europe and Jews became the scapegoat for Germany's discontent

committee and discovered that four of the seven members were Jewish. He doesn't say how he did this. It might have been mere bravado on his part, or he might simply have assumed that those whose surnames sounded Jewish must have been Jews. He then claimed to have written a spiteful letter to the director ending with the threat, 'For this the Jews will pay!' [7]

Seething with resentment he now turned his energies on those he imagined had denied him his calling and in doing so, ironically and tragically, secured his place in history.

PERVERTED PHILOSOPHY

'I suddenly encountered an apparition in a black caftan and black sidelocks. "Is this a Jew?" was my first thought. For, to be sure, they had not looked like that in Linz. I observed the man furtively and cautiously, but the longer I stared at this foreign face, scrutinizing feature for feature, the more my first question assumed a new form. "Was this a German?"'

Adolf Hitler, *Mein Kampf*

Hitler's first encounter with an orthodox Jew in Vienna awakened his innate paranoia and provided him with an entire race on to which he could project his feelings of unworthiness and his morbid sexual obsessions.

'Wherever I went I began to see Jews and the more I saw, the more sharply they became distinguished in my eyes from the rest of humanity... I began to hate them... I had ceased to be a weak-kneed cosmopolitan and became an anti-Semite.'

It is a mistake to imagine that Hitler formed his racist ideology after studying the great German philosophers such as Nietzsche, Hegel and Luther. He lacked the intellectual capacity to follow their arguments and was certainly incapable of formulating philosophical theories of his own. Moreover, he had no patience for literature, preferring to amuse himself with the children's adventure stories of Rabautz the horse and the popular westerns of Karl May. Contrary to claims by Kubizek that Adolf was an avid reader (a claim he subsequently retracted) there were no books of 'humane or intellectual value' in his library, according to Christa Schroeder, one of the Führer's private secretaries.

Nor did Hitler quote from the likes of Hegel and Nietzsche in his memoirs, speeches or informal table talks, an omission which betrayed the fact that he simply wasn't familiar with them. All of his ideas were obtained second-hand from the most specious of sources – the anti-Semitic pamphlets and racist periodicals 'bought for a few pennies' during his Vienna days, which served to reinforce his prejudices and gratify his craving for pornography. It is

Portrait of the mystic Guido von List

clear from the hysterical nature of the texts, from the crude cartoons and lurid illustrations, that these publications were not political tracts but were intended to satisfy the sadistic and sexual appetites of their male readers.

It has been argued that Hitler was also influenced by the *völkisch* 'mystics' Lanz von Liebenfels (1874–1954) and Guido von List (1865–1919), as well as the other pseudo-intellectuals who adopted aristocratic names to hide their working class origins. But he doesn't appear to have understood their convoluted reasoning – he merely regurgitated it. The parallels between List, Liebenfels and Hitler are strikingly similar, so much so that there can be little doubt that Hitler simply used his impressive facility for retaining facts to commit to memory whole passages from his mentors' manifestos.

[For more on List and Liebenfels see the author's *Nazis and the Occult*, Arcturus 2007.]

PREJUDICE AND PLAGIARISM

In 1934, for example, Hitler first considered the ways in which Germany could prevent 'racial decay' and then suggested, 'shall we form an Order, the Brotherhood of Templars round the Holy Grail of the pure blood?' It was a phrase which echoed almost word for word that of his dark guru Liebenfels who had written in 1913 of, 'The Holy Grail of German blood that must be defended by the Brotherhood of the Templars'. Hitler also stole key phrases from List and Liebenfels such as 'the Hydra-headed international Jewish conspiracy', which appeared with monotonous regularity in his speeches and informal rants.

Liebenfels' anti-Semitic and *völkisch* theories were spread all over the pages of his magazine *Ostara*, of which Hitler was an avid reader. The anti-Semitic Viennese newspaper, *Deutsche Volksblatt*, also fuelled Hitler's rhetoric of hatred. But Hitler found more than political and racist doggerel in the rancid pages of *Ostara* and the *Volksblatt*. Hysterical, ill-informed articles on the subjects of women's rights, homo-sexuality, syphilis and castration provided him with the justification for his fear of intimacy. 'Evidence' in the form of cranial diagrams was presented in support of the pamphleteer's belief that women were intellectually inferior and that 'over-educated race murdering educational idiots and characterless professors' could be identified by the shape of their skulls.

Readers were encouraged to take *Ostara's* racial biology test which allotted points according to physical characteristics. There were 12 points to be had for blue eyes, while, predictably, points were deducted for dark eyes. Tall, blond, white-skinned males with the 'right shaped nose' earned top marks (women were ineligible) and were deemed to be the Aryan ideal, those in the middle range with a total score below 100 were designated 'mixed breeds' and those falling below zero were condemned as 'apelings'.

One can only imagine what Hitler must have thought of Liebenfels' assertion that 'The most important and decisive erotic force for people of the higher race is the eye.'

ARYANS AND ATLANTIS

Both List and Liebenfels declared that the accepted view of history was wrong and that the Teutonic people were the descendants of a superior race known as the Aryans, who had survived the destruction of their homeland of Atlantis at the time of the Flood. According to the revisionist vision of the two 'mystics', the Aryans had lost their intellectual and physical powers through interbreeding with primitive inferior beings over several millennia. It was therefore their duty to restore themselves to their rightful place as the Master Race by driving the *Untermenschen* (subhumans) from Europe – thereby preserving the purity of their bloodline. List and Liebenfels predicted that this New Order would be ushered in with the arrival of a Messiah who would lead the German people in a final apocalyptic battle with the inferior races – specifically the Slavs, the negroes and the Jews, whom Liebenfels referred to as the 'Dark Ones'. List prophesied that 'the Aryo-German demands a self-chosen Führer to whom he willingly submits'. If that is true the German people got the leader they wished for and deserved. Amazingly, this preposterous juvenile fantasy

circulated as fact in Germany and Austria in the years preceding the First World War.

By embracing the mythology of the *völkisch* 'mystics' (for they liked to think of themselves as such, though they had no serious spiritual values of any kind), Hitler wrapped himself in a mantle of pseudo-philosophy and respectability and finally found a focus for his neurosis. He also acquired a potent symbol which was to become the emblem of the Nazi Party and its brutality – the swastika. Both List and Liebenfels advocated the adoption of the

Start them young: swastikas proliferated as Nazi ideology led Germans from the cradle to the grave

April 1936, and members of the Baker's Union in Berlin look rather solemn as they display the fruit of their labours, a giant cake to celebrate the Führer's 47th birthday

Hakenkreuz (hooked cross) as the emblem of Aryan might (an ancient Nordic symbol of the primal fire from which the universe evolved), while List promoted the double sig rune of the Nordic alphabet as the symbol of racial purity – a symbol that was to be adopted as the insignia of the hated SS.

Another pernicious influence on the young

Hitler was racist 'philosopher' Theodor Fritsch (1852–1934), whose *Handbook of the Jewish Question* he 'studied intensively'. Again, the text was not on the same intellectual level as Nietzsche or Hegel. It was merely a collection of short essays accusing Jews of the worst crimes in history, together with a section of anti-Semitic sound bites attributed to famous

'I AM THE GERMAN MAN. I AM THE GERMAN SPIRIT.'
Richard Wagner

authors, which the pocket-sized politician would have committed to memory to endorse his own views. Fritsch's rabid attack on Heine, the 19th century poet and essayist, is indeed typical of his warped logic.

'In Heine two forces are noticeably fighting each other. It is as though a piece of Teutonic spirit within him is attempting to ascend to more ideal heights, until the Jew suddenly pulls him down again by the legs into the morass where he then wallows with delight and jeers at all ideals.'

What is particularly noteworthy about Fritsch is his frenzied attack on Freud, whom he accuses of setting out to 'destroy the German soul… and the German family'. Hitler would have seized on that idea in particular as it undermined the authority and insights of the emerging science of psychoanalysis, which would have made a man with his catalogue of complexes decidedly uncomfortable.

WAGNER

Perhaps the most insidious influence of all on the nihilistic ideology of Adolf Hitler and his Nazi Party was that of the composer Richard Wagner (1813–83). Wagner was undoubtedly a musical genius but as a man he was, by all accounts, as abhorrent as Hitler. In fact, both men shared many of the same characteristics, so much so that one is bound to ask if Hitler's admiration was intensified by his personal identification with his idol. As Hitler himself admitted, 'I have the most intimate familiarity with Wagner's mental processes.'[8]

Both men were intolerably opinionated and self-obsessed and both were enamoured of the sound of their own voices. They considered themselves experts on a wide variety of subjects, but their writings and recorded conversations reveal that they only had a superficial understanding of what they were discussing and could offer no insights of value. As Robert Waite, author of *The Psychopathic God*, has noted, if their reputations and influence had depended on their written works alone they would have been dismissed as racist cranks. Waite also notes that both men also wrote 'execrable prose', which was so convoluted and grammatically poor that their translators were often forced to capitulate and fall back on the original German.

The fault testified to their irrational mode of thinking rather than their lack of education – though in Hitler's case his atrocious grammar and spelling remained remarkably poor for a modern political leader.

Waite suggests that both men might have affected an exaggerated macho image in order to disguise their latent homosexuality. Wagner dressed up in pink silk gowns and composed amidst clouds of perfume, while Hitler wielded a riding crop – he once beat his dog with it in an effort to impress a female admirer. Both men also displayed childlike abandon when they were pleased and attention-seeking temper tantrums when they couldn't get their own way. But perhaps the most significant obsession they shared was their suspicion that their real fathers were Jews. In order to exorcise that fear they denounced the Jews more vehemently than any other anti-Semites. In neither case was their

Jewish parentage ever proven, but the possibility tormented them to the end of their days.

A TURBULENT NATURE

Beneath all the nationalistic pomp and pageantry of Wagner's operas, which extolled German virtues and heroism, was his obsession with incest and cloying mother-love. Such themes and undertones, which bordered on the oedipal, would not have been lost on Hitler, for whom Wagner's music was both quasi-religious and emotionally therapeutic. As Kubizek observed, 'Wagner's music produced in him that escape into a mystical dream world which he needed in order to endure the tensions of his turbulent nature.'

The racist pamphleteers had politicized the young Hitler but Wagner's talk of the advent of a German hero had inflamed him with a missionary zeal. There would be a new Barbarossa, Wagner said, who would restore German honour and sweep aside parliamentary democracy, which he dismissed as a Franco-Judaic deceit. Man was a beast of prey, Wagner wrote, and great civilizations were founded on conquest and the subjugation of weaker races.

Although Wagner apologists maintain that his ravings should not deter us from enjoying his music, it has to be remembered that it was Wagner who first proposed the idea of a 'final solution' to the 'Jewish Question'. There can be little doubt about what he was proposing because he talked about a time when there would be no more Jews, whom he called 'the enemy of mankind'.

Such was the self-indulgent rant of the artist who can afford to live in a fantasy world of his own making, but Hitler took his idol at his word and swore to lead this struggle between Teutonic supermen and subhumans, or perish in the process.

THE DESERTER

The immediate result of Hitler's exposure to racist pamphlets was to enrol himself and his friend Kubizek in the Austrian Antisemitic League. To Hitler, Vienna was no longer the cultural capital of his homeland but a 'racist Babylon' seething with Jews.

But before he could begin preaching his new faith he learned that he was to be arrested by the Austro-Hungarian Army for evading conscription. In May 1913 he fled to Munich where he found comfortable well-furnished rooms above a tailor's shop in Schwabing, the artistic district, for just 20 marks a month. His average income at the time was 100 marks a month, which more than catered for his daily needs. He obtained it by selling his paintings for between 10 and 20 marks each. It was, by his own admission, 'the happiest and most contented' period of his life. But on 18 January of the following year the Austrian authorities finally caught up with him. He was arrested as a deserter and taken to the Austrian-Hungarian consulate to explain his failure to report for duty.

Hitler must have presented a pathetic spectacle, and played the part of the *Nebbish* (sincere but harmless fool) to the hilt, because he succeeded in persuading the Consul General that he was 'deserving of considerate treatment'. He was freed on condition that he report to the Military Commission in Salzburg for assessment. On 5 February 1914 the commission declared him unfit for military service due to an unspecified complaint and he was dismissed.

He returned to his easy life and his rooms above the tailor's shop until August, when the old world of empires came to a sudden and violent end.

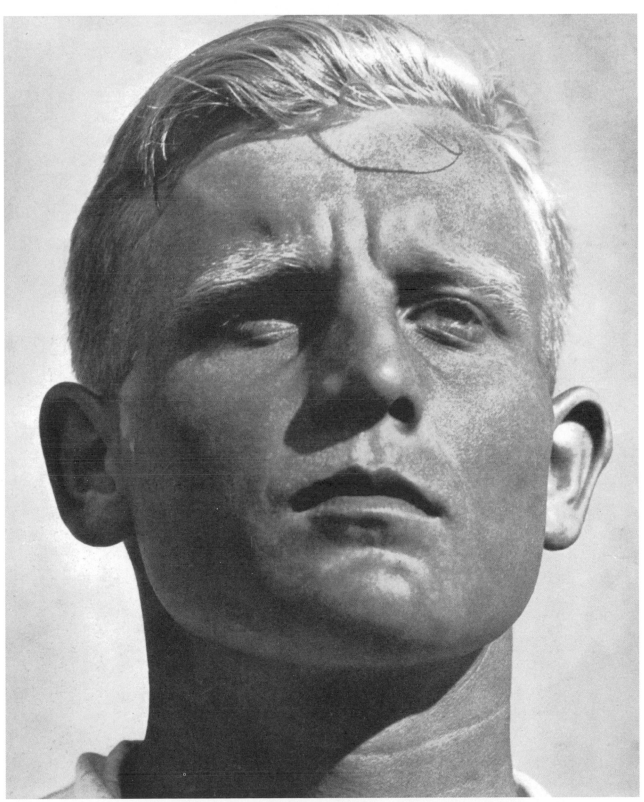

Tomorrow belongs to me: portrait of a Hitler Youth member who represents the ideal Aryan type so beloved of the Nazis' racist ideology and which Hitler himself so little resembled

CHAPTER FOUR

TURBULENT TIMES

WAR DECLARED

There is a famous photograph taken of the crowd in Munich's Odeonplatz on the day that war was declared in August 1914. Among the thousands of cheering people is the 25-year-old Adolf Hitler, captured in a moment of euphoria. His fellow citizens doubtless shared his patriotism and the belief that the coming war was just and could well be over by Christmas. But for Hitler the approaching conflict was not solely about avenging the assassination of the Austrian Archduke or standing by an ally: it was a 'deliverance' from a monotonous, aimless life and as such it empowered him with a sense of purpose.

'To me those hours came as a deliverance from the distress that had weighed upon me during the days of my youth. I am not ashamed to say that, carried away by the enthusiasm of the moment, I sank down on my knees and thanked heaven out of the fullness of my heart for granting me the good fortune of being permitted to live in such a time.'[9]

The war also gave him a sense of identity and the opportunity to avenge the violation of his motherland.

Hitler had a 'good' war by all accounts. He earned a promotion to corporal in the List Regiment and his bravery earned him an Iron Cross Second Class in 1914 and an Iron Cross First Class in 1918, but his comrades disliked him. He was not promoted to a higher rank because the officers knew that the men would not follow his orders.

THE WHITE CROW

There was something odd in Hitler's demeanour that led his comrades to shun him. One recalled that he looked at his rifle 'with delight, as a woman looks at her jewellery'. They called him the 'white crow' because he never laughed or joked unless it was in response to the misfortunes of others. Hitler despised his comrades for their lack of patriotism and their disrespect for their officers and they in turn distrusted him because he kept himself aloof and didn't make an effort to join in.

There was something unsettling in his compulsive cleanliness, which amounted to a mania, and his almost religious aversion to smoking, drinking and women. He was known in the battalion as 'the woman hater' and would habitually lecture them on the dangers of interracial intercourse. At every opportunity he would hold forth on the evils of Marxism, Freemasonry and

Face in the crowd: the jubilant Hitler is pictured in the crowd as war is announced in 1914

On the margins: Hitler (left, marked by cross) with his fellow soldiers during World War I. He remained aloof from his comrades, feeling they lacked respect for their officers and the Motherland

the International Jewish Conspiracy to the amusement of his comrades, who would deliberately provoke him in order to relieve the tedium of trench life.

'We all cursed him and found him intolerable', recalled one comrade, who was disconcerted by Hitler's uncanny knack for evading certain death. Time and again he would escape unscathed from a heavy bombardment or emerge unharmed from a skirmish in which others had been killed or wounded.

The letters and postcards he wrote from the front are stiff and formal, revealing nothing of the writer's character – only his

'THE LIGHTS ARE GOING OUT ALL OVER EUROPE. I DO NOT KNOW IF WE SHALL SEE THEM LIT AGAIN IN OUR LIFETIME.'

Edward Grey, 1st Viscount Grey of Fallodon [10]

obsessions. In his correspondence to his landlord, and the baker who offended his sensibilities by sending a food parcel, Hitler warns of 'a world of enemies' and repeats his unwavering belief that he had been miraculously spared in order to fulfil a special mission. There is no hint of humanity, only of his neurosis.

Even after being wounded in the shoulder by shrapnel in October 1916, Hitler begged to be able to return to the front so that he could spend Christmas alone there at headquarters, where he served as a runner. Ever since his mother had died he had ensured that he was alone at

Hitler in his field uniform around 1915: close calls with death fed his sense of destiny

Christmas, a practice he continued even after his rise to power. Alone on the most festive day of the year he could play the martyr to the hilt.

STABBED IN THE BACK

When the armistice was announced in November 1918 Hitler was in Pasewalk Hospital, Pomerania, where he was recovering from the effects of chlorine gas inhaled during the battle of Ypres the previous month. Defeat was something he simply could not comprehend, despite the fact that the Allies now had the Americans on their side. It was intolerable to think that Germany had capitulated after all the privation and sacrifice it had endured.

'Everything began to go black again before my eyes. Stumbling, I groped my way back to the ward, threw myself on my bed and buried my burning head in the covers and pillows. I had not cried since the day I had stood at the grave of my mother.'

It was then that the myth of the 'November Criminals' was born. German soldiers who could not bring themselves to believe that their almighty armed forces had been defeated began to talk of being 'stabbed in the back' by defeatists at home.

'We could have brought the struggle to a favourable conclusion if… co-operation had existed between the army and those at home. But while the enemy showed an even greater will for victory, divergent party interests began to show themselves with us… No blame is to be attached to the sound core of the army… It is plain enough with whom the blame lies.' (General Hindenburg, November 1919)

VERSAILLES

The excessively harsh terms of the Versailles Treaty, which imposed punitive reparations on Germany in June 1919, prepared the ground in which extreme nationalism and the bitter fruit of fanaticism were to take root. The terms, which included the loss of all overseas colonies, the surrender of Alsace-Lorraine to France and the occupation of the strategically vital Saar region and the Rhineland, were clearly intended to punish and humiliate Germany, which was required to accept all the blame for the hostilities.

In total, 13 per cent of German territory was taken by the victors, which meant that overnight 6 million Germans lost their citizenship. On top of that, 20 per cent of the German coal, iron and steel industry was appropriated by the victors and the German army was reduced to 100,000 men – a force that would have been insufficient to defend Berlin. The greater part of the German navy was seized by the British and Germany was forbidden to possess submarines, tanks and heavy artillery and prohibited from developing an air force. In effect, Germany was stripped of her assets, denied the means of defending herself and billed for the damage and suffering it had caused – which was valued at £6,600 million in 1921.

The terms of the treaty were not negotiable. It was, as the French say, a *fait accompli*, or a *Diktat* as the Germans termed it (a dictated peace). To add insult to the perceived injury, Germany was also denied membership of the newly formed League of Nations, which implied that the nation as a whole was not to be trusted even in such a co-operative venture.

BIRTH OF A REPUBLIC

'Extreme times call for extreme measures.' Such was the sentiment with which millions of German citizens rationalized their decision to vote for the Nazi Party in the 1920s – and with some justification. In the aftermath of the First World War Germany was tearing itself to pieces. During the last weeks of the war the generals had persuaded Kaiser Wilhelm ll to transfer power to the Reichstag (the German parliament) so that they could blame the politicians for their defeat. On 3 October 1918 Prince Max von Baden formed a new government and that same day asked the Allies for an armistice. The

Depression and despair: after World War I, Berlin was destitute and the mood was sombre. Soon there was fighting on the streets between left and right, and the Nazis began to gear up for power

A nation in uproar: revolutionary soldiers and sailors are shown keeping crowds under control in 1919 during a demonstration outside the Imperial Palace

German people were stunned by the sudden capitulation, having believed the press reports which stated that just 'one more push' was needed to ensure final victory.

The immediate reaction of the troops was to mutiny. Sailors took over the port at Wilhelmshaven and the navy base at Kiel, as well as other key installations around the country, while hastily elected councils comprising soldiers and workers seized control of the major cities. In Bavaria left-wing radicals declared a socialist republic and a series of strikes and demonstrations brought Berlin to a standstill. Then in an effort to restore order the Kaiser abdicated and a new government under Friedrich Ebert was formed. In January 1919 elections were held for a new National Assembly and in the following month the members met in the town of Weimar, after which Ebert declared that Imperialist Germany

was no more. The country was now a republic and he was its president.

AN EPIDEMIC OF EXTREMISM

But the birth of the republic was a difficult one, to say the least. For the first five years of its life it witnessed a succession of armed revolutions and attempted coups as extremists on all sides of the political spectrum struggled violently for control. The government's answer was to form the Freikorps – armed volunteers acting under orders from former army officers. They were allowed to run riot and shoot anyone they suspected of supporting the insurgents. It was anarchy on the streets with the army on one side and the workers on the other. Transport and communications were brought to a standstill in an effort to force the Freikorps to stand down. This intolerable situation culminated in the so-called Kapp Putsch of March 1920, which only ended when millions of German workers downed tools. That was enough to force the leaders of the uprising, Wolfgang Kapp and General von Luttwitz, to flee to Sweden.

Ebert then demanded that the Freikorps be disbanded, which only inflamed the right-wing radicals. They vowed to fight on, to which end they formed underground organizations and assassination squads, which led to 354 murders taking place by the end of 1923. It is not true to say that Hitler and the Nazis were solely responsible for inciting right-wing extremism in Germany at that time for extreme nationalism had already reached epidemic proportions in the Weimar Republic. One wit described it as 'a republic with few republicans'.

The army as a whole was sympathetic to the right and so could not be relied upon to support the government, while the judges treated right-wing extremists with extraordinary leniency, undermining the rule of law.

The situation was made even more intolerable by the fact that after 1920 the republic was ruled by coalition governments that were not only constantly in disagreement but were also struggling to keep the Communists and Nationalists from exerting any influence on policy. It is not surprising that in such a volatile and unstable situation the cry went out for a 'strong man' to bring order from chaos.

In 1925 the ageing Field Marshal Paul von Hindenburg was elected president of the republic in an effort to restore confidence in the administration. However, it was no secret that Hindenburg was not a supporter of the republic but in fact favoured the restoration of the monarchy and the return of the Kaiser. In this he was supported by the Nationalists, who were then the second-largest party in parliament, as well as the civil service, the industrialists, the judges and, most significantly, the army.

AN ABSURD LITTLE ORGANIZATION

Many men who survived the horrors of trench warfare returned bitter and disillusioned from the so called 'war to end wars', but Hitler returned to Munich more embittered than most. Not only was his belief in German supremacy shattered, but he subscribed to the myth that the true reason for defeat lay not on the battlefield, nor even back at headquarters, but with the anonymous cabal of conspirators who had no backbone for continuing the war of attrition. Being a paranoiac he took this betrayal personally and vowed revenge. He did not have long to wait, for in September 1919 his army superiors assigned him to report on a small political party. The idea was that he would attend meetings in the capacity of *Vertrauensmann* (the army's 'trusted representative').

'This was a time in which anyone who was not satisfied with developments… felt called upon to found a new party. Everywhere these organizations sprang out of the ground, only to vanish silently after a time. I judged the German Workers' Party no differently.'

'THIS WAS A TIME IN WHICH ANYONE WHO WAS NOT SATISFIED WITH DEVELOPMENTS… FELT CALLED UPON TO FOUND A NEW PARTY.'

The Deutsche Arbeiterpartei was a ragged collective of backstreet radicals with a racist agenda, a membership of less than 60 and few prospects of making an impression on local politics. It had been founded by Anton Drexler, a railway engineer, and Karl Harrer, a journalist, with the intention of creating a national movement that would improve the lot of the workers. However, neither of them had a talent for public speaking or organization.

Hitler had chosen to attend a meeting in the Sterneckerbrau beer keller in the city's Tal district, where the DAP had invited a self-appointed expert in economics to talk on the subject of 'interest slavery'. When he had finished, a member of the audience rose to argue the case for Bavarian sovereignty, which was a thorny but topical issue at the time. This incensed Hitler, who emerged from the shadows to shout him down. It was his unassailable conviction rather than the force of his argument that impressed Drexler, Harrer and the small audience. All agreed that Hitler was an impressive, emotive speaker with an intimidating manner that permitted no disagreement.

When the meeting ended Drexler pressed a pamphlet into Hitler's hand entitled 'My Political Awakening'. The next morning Hitler read it with interest as he lay on his cot back at the barracks.

Later that same day he received a written invitation to join the party, but at that time he didn't have any intention of doing so. He later claimed that he had been seriously thinking about forming his own political party and had only attended a second meeting in order to tell the committee that he had no intention of joining their 'absurd little organization'.

At that second meeting, in the Alte Rosenbad in the Herrenstrasse, the pitiful state of the party's funds was being discussed amid the odour of strong beer and stale cigarette smoke. As Hitler later recalled in *Mein Kampf*: 'In the grim light of a tiny gas lamp four people were sitting at a table… The minutes of the last meeting were read and the secretary gave a vote of confidence. Next came the treasury report – all in all the party possessed seven marks and fifty pfennigs – for which the treasurer received a vote of confidence. This too was entered into the minutes… Terrible, terrible! This was club life of the worst sort. Was I to join such an organization?'

In his highly embellished account of that fateful meeting, Hitler described how he struggled with his conscience for days before deciding to join, but that he finally submitted to fate. In fact, he was ordered to join the party by his superior, Lieutenant Mayr, who realized that the right-wing organization had the potential to attract ex-soldiers and workers away from the Communists, who were seen as a threat to the army and the stability of the German state.

SEIZING THE MOMENT

In January 1920 Hitler was enrolled as the 55th member of the DAP. This was later altered to number 7 so that it would look as if he had been in at the beginning. Another early member was the playwright Dietrich Eckhart, whose morphine and alcohol addiction had earned him an enforced stay in a mental institution, where he managed to entice the inmates into staging his plays. Eckhart was an early and significant influence on Hitler. He coached him in the art of public speaking, rewrote his speeches and articles to improve his poor grammar and introduced him to his wealthy friends, who became

'The Word': propaganda painting of Hitler speaking in the Sterneckerbrau – from such small beginnings, he expanded the Nazi Party organization until it became the ruling entity

patrons of the party in the hope that their interests would be served. But Eckhart did not live to see the party take power. He died three years later, an unrepentant addict. His last words were to take on a meaning that he could not possibly have foreseen.

'Do not mourn me for I shall have influenced history more than any other German.'

During the first few months of his membership Hitler busied himself typing invitations to meetings that took place in a gloomy back room at the Sterneckerbrau, only to watch as the same seven members took their places in the empty hall. Frustrated, he placed an advert in a local newspaper and was thrilled when more than a hundred people turned up. He was so delighted that he ignored Harrer's objections and gave an impromptu speech, which was greeted enthusiastically. The next month, to the horror of his

fellow committee members, Hitler organized a meeting at the Hofbrauhaus, which could seat 2,000. Harrer was so infuriated that he resigned, later claiming that it was Hitler's anti-Semitism that had forced his hand. But to everyone's surprise the meeting was a huge success. The guest speaker was yet another eccentric economic 'expert' and his theories were greeted with a stony silence by the increasingly restless audience. Seizing the moment, Hitler rose to his feet and began a tirade against the 'November Criminals' and the Jews.

'There was a hail of shouts, there were violent clashes in the hall… After half an hour the applause began to drown out the screaming and shouting… When, after nearly four hours, the hall began to empty I knew that now the principles of the movement which could no longer be forgotten were moving out among the German people.'

The party was then renamed – it became the National Socialist German Workers' Party (Nationalsozialistische Deutsche Arbeiterpartei or NSDAP, from which came the word 'Nazi'). Its manifesto, part of which can be seen here, was drawn largely from Hitler's speech on that day, 24 February 1920.

Programme of the National Socialist German Workers' Party

1. We demand on the basis of the right of national self-determination the union of all Germans in a Greater Germany.
2. We demand equality for the German nation among other nations and the revocation of the peace treaty of Versailles and Saint Germain.
3. We demand land (colonies) to feed our people and to settle our excess population.
4. Only a racial comrade can be a citizen. Only a person of German blood irrespective of religious denomination can be a racial comrade. No Jew therefore can be a racial comrade.
5. Non-citizens shall be able to live in Germany as guests only and must be placed under alien legislation.
6. We therefore demand that every public office no matter what kind and no matter whether it be national, state or local office be held by none but citizens. We oppose the corrupting parliamentary custom of making party considerations and not 'character and ability' the criterion for appointments to official positions.
7. We demand that the state make it its primary duty to provide a livelihood for its citizens. If it should prove impossible to feed the entire population the members of foreign nations (non-citizens) are to be expelled from Germany.
8. Any further immigration of non-Germans is to be prevented. We demand all non-Germans that enter Germany after 2 August 1914 be forced to leave the Reich without delay.
9. All citizens are to possess equal rights and obligations.
10. It must be the first duty of every citizen to perform mental or physical work. Individual activity must not violate the general interest and must be exercised within the frame of the community and for the general good.

Among the remaining 15 points of the manifesto were promises to end all sources of unearned income (that is, interest on savings and share dividends), to confiscate war profits, to nationalize corporations and department stores, to bring about wholesale health and education reform and to place the press under state control, for it was said to be run exclusively by 'racial comrades'. No one could say they had not been warned. Even in those early days the party made no attempt to hide its rabid racism. The manifesto ended with a demand for a 'strong central power' with 'unconditional authority over the entire Reich'.[11]

In the summer of 1920 Hitler adopted the swastika as the symbol of the NSDAP. What had once been an emblem of unity in the esoteric tradition now became the insignia of fanaticism. It is thought that Hitler must have seen it used as the emblem of the Austrian anti-Semitic parties, or possibly emblazoned on the helmets of the Freikorps who marched into Munich to put down the Kapp Putsch.

MONEY, MONEY, MONEY

If any single factor can be said to have tipped the scales in favour of the Nazis during the Weimar years it was the rampant inflation which saw ordinary Germans paying for a loaf of bread with what had once been a month's wages. Customers wheeling wheelbarrows piled high with almost worthless Reichmarks became a common sight in German towns and cities, a sight that literally brought home to ordinary citizens the precarious nature of their economy and the ineffectiveness of their government. Wages were devalued overnight and savings were wiped out. Employers were forced to pay their workers twice a day so that they could buy food and drink for their families before the mark lost more of its value.

The problem had been created by the Kaiser, who had borrowed heavily to fund the war, but it was exacerbated by the Republican government who printed more money than the economy could handle in order to balance their books. By the spring of 1923 they were spending seven times more than they received in revenue, having been forced to buy coal from abroad. The Ruhr had been occupied by the French since the German government had admitted that it could not afford to make further reparation payments.

In July 1914 four marks were roughly equivalent to one US dollar. By the end of the war twice as many marks were needed to buy one dollar. By January 1923 one dollar would buy nearly 18,000 marks and by the end of that year one dollar was worth 4.2 billion marks. In December 1918 one mark would buy two loaves of bread. By December 1922 one loaf cost 165 marks and within a year the price of a loaf had risen to 1,500,000 marks. Germans lost patience with their elected representatives and in their panic believed that anything was better than this. In such a state they were prepared to set aside any criticisms they might have had of Nazi 'excess' and were willing to give these extreme nationalists a chance.

Whatever the source, Hitler was shrewd enough to wrap his new symbol in the trappings of tradition by placing the black-hooked cross in a white circle bordered by red – the colours of old Imperial Prussia.

'In red we see the social ideal of the movement, in white the nationalist idea, in the swastika the mission of the struggle for the victory of Aryan man.'

But few were fooled, for soon afterwards the Nazis revealed their true colours by staging the disastrous Munich Putsch.

THE HITLER GANG

Rudolf Hess was the first of Hitler's acolytes to join the party. He had served with Hitler in the Great War, but had failed to make an impression on his future leader. It was only after he had heard Hitler speak at a rally in 1921, and had presented him with an essay extolling the

Party time: in 1936 the NSDAP held their annual meeting in Munich's opera house. In the front row are members of the Nazis' inner sanctum, including Hess, Goebbels, Hitler and Goering

qualities of the ideal German leader, that he was welcomed into the fold. He wrote, 'Only a man of the people can establish authority… He himself has nothing in common with the mass; like every great man he is all personality… When necessity commands, he does not shrink before bloodshed… In order to reach his goal he is prepared to trample on his closest friends…'

Hitler was suitably flattered to see himself portrayed in such terms and immediately offered the 26-year-old former economics student the role of secretary. Hess was beside himself with joy, like a man 'overcome by a vision'. He returned home to his wife repeating over and over 'The man! The man!' He had found the master he had been born to serve.

It is tempting to compare beetle-browed Hess' relationship with Hitler, the master

mesmerist, to that of the cataleptic Cesare with Caligari in that classic of German silent expressionist cinema, *The Cabinet of Dr Caligari*. The film is set in a fairground where Cesare, a somnambulist, is exhibited by Dr Caligari. At night, still fast asleep, Cesare silently murders the nearby town's inhabitants under the orders of his master.

In fact, one of Hess' professors at Munich University described his pupil's disconcerting stare as 'somnambulistic' and recalled that Hess was uncommonly 'slow' and 'dull'. Hitler valued Hess' unquestioning obedience and his deference, but admitted that he found him a tedious companion.

'Every conversation with Hess becomes an unbearably tormenting strain,' Hitler said.

He used Hess as he used everyone else that came into his sphere of influence, but he despised his deputy's lack of interest in art and culture. He also thought that Hess' obsession with eccentric alternative therapies, biodynamic diets and esoteric ideas such as astrology was symptomatic of a confused and disordered mind.

Hermann Goering was an altogether more formidable figure. A former fighter pilot in Baron von Richthofen's famous squadron he saw himself as a war hero, an aristocrat and a big game hunter. But he was more interested in acquiring medals and new uniforms than winning the war. His jovial, avuncular image hid a mean, vindictive nature, which led him to carry a small black book in which he recorded, for future reckoning, the names of anyone who offended him. It was Goering who established the first concentration camps and it was Goering

A silhouette feared by many: Hermann Goering at Berlin's Sportpalast in 1935

again who created the Gestapo. After joining the party in 1921 his first position was deputy of the SA (Sturm Abteilung, or 'brownshirts'), but he soon rose to the position of deputy leader. The only man he feared was Hitler who promised him an active and prominent role in the coming fight.

'I joined the party because I was a revolutionary,' Goering boasted, 'not because of some ideological nonsense.'

Barely five feet (1.5 metres) tall and disabled by a distinct limp, Dr Paul Joseph Goebbels was not the most imposing figure in the party, but he was a formidable personality. A caustic, sharp-tongued master of manipulation, his enemies nicknamed him 'the poison dwarf'. He had studied at eight universities before finally receiving his doctorate, after which he had tried and failed to establish himself as a playwright and journalist. But he found his calling when he heard Hitler speak at the Circus Krone in Munich in June 1922.

'At that moment I was reborn!' he exclaimed.

When Hitler was imprisoned in Landsberg

Public display of unity: in private Hitler complained his subordinate Hess was a crank

Joseph Goebbels in the company of a Hitler Youth: the Minister of Propaganda could, he claimed, play the popular will like a piano, making the German people all dance to his tune

after the Beer Hall Putsch (see below), Goebbels wrote him a gushing letter that was intended to make the leader remember his name.

'Like a rising star you appeared before our wondering eyes, you performed miracles to clear our minds and, in a world of scepticism and desperation, gave us faith… You named the need of a whole generation… One day Germany will thank you.'

He followed his Führer's career with interest from that day on, but always from the sidelines, because his socialist views were at odds with Hitler's own. In particular, Goebbels believed that the state had a right to the land and wealth left behind by the royal family. It was an issue he was prepared to defend in a public debate with his idol. At Bamberg on 14 February 1926 he got his wish, but it was Hitler's personal magnetism and powers of persuasion that appear to have finally converted Dr Goebbels,

rather than the logic of his argument. Goebbels' diary entry for April 13 reveals the depth of his devotion

'[Hitler] can make you doubt your own views… I am now at ease about him… I bow to the greater man, to the political genius.'

In October 1926 Hitler rewarded his 'faithful, unshakable shield bearer' by appointing the 29-year-old Goebbels to the position of *Gauleiter* (district leader) for Berlin, with orders to rein in the rabid brutes of the SA and rout the Communists from the capital. Goebbels gave Hitler his assurance that he would not disappoint him.

Without doubt the most sinister figure in the Nazi inner circle was Heinrich Himmler, former secretary to Gregor Strasser, who became head of the SS, Hitler's praetorian guard, in 1929. He was just 28 years old. At that time the bespectacled bureaucrat commanded just 200 men, but within four years he would increase that figure to 50,000 and introduce a tough selection programme that would ensure that the black-uniformed troops were seen as the elite. Ironically the wiry hypochondriac would not have fulfilled his own entry criteria because he suffered from poor eyesight and chronic stomach complaints and was said to become sick at the sight of blood. But Himmler, like Hitler, intended that others would do his killing for him.

To compensate for his physical shortcomings, Himmler developed a mystical side in which he believed himself to be the reincarnation of King Henry the Fowler, founder of the First Reich. As a result, he could claim that his strength came from the spirit – something that no one could test and find wanting.

Other leading lights in the party in the early days included the crackpot 'philosopher' Alfred Rosenberg, who replaced the ailing

Alfred Rosenberg was a notorious anti-Semite with a seminal influence on Nazi ideology

Eckhart as editor of the party newspaper. 'Hitler values me a great deal, but he does not like me,' he freely admitted.

Rosenberg's reputation rested on being the author of the vile anti-Semitic tome *The Myth of the 20th Century*, which rivals *Mein Kampf* for the distinction of being the bestselling unread book in history.

BACK ROOM RADICALS

From the moment Hitler took the floor at party meetings no one was allowed to upstage him. Opposition was not tolerated. Dissent was drowned in the torrent of words that burst forth from him as if a dam had been breached. Hitler had found his voice and his platform, the party had its new spokesman and its fortunes were assured.

An early supporter of the party, Kurt Ludecke, described the hold Hitler exercised over his audience in those days.

Heinrich Himmler (4th from left, front row) saw himelf as regent in a kind of Nazi Camelot

Hitler walks ahead of Ernst Röhm as they sweep by Nazi flag companies at Franzen Feld, Brunswick. The thuggish Röhm promised his men free beer and uniforms and as much action as they could handle

'When he spoke of the disgrace of Germany I felt ready to spring on any enemy… I experienced an exultation that could be likened only to religious conversion.'

But Hitler's increasing influence in the party was not entirely due to the power of his personality. The members were impressed by the infusion of almost unlimited funds that his army paymasters had put at his disposal, provided he took control of the organization.

Hitler's rabble-rousing speeches began to attract large numbers of right-wing sympathisers to the monthly meetings in the Munich beer keller, but supporters of the Communist opposition also crowded into the back of the smoke-filled hall. They were intent on disrupting proceedings. Fist fights and barracking became a regular feature, which Hitler determined to stamp out by recruiting what was euphemistically described as a security detail. The SA (Sturmabteilung) were recruited by Ernst Röhm, a bull-necked ex-army thug. He promised his men free beer and uniforms and as much action as they could handle. But Hitler had another reason for wanting to surround himself with muscle. The SA would serve to intimidate the opposition when he felt the time was right to make his play for leadership of the party. The ranks of the brown-shirted storm troopers swelled almost as rapidly as the audience, which was now treated to Hitler's speeches uninterrupted. All opposition was ruthlessly silenced in the alley at the back of the beer hall as Hitler's words rang out.

'The SA is intended to bind our young party members together to form an organization of iron, so that it may put its strength at the disposal of the whole movement to act as a battering ram.' [12]

Hitler was more explicit when he described the part the SA was to play in the coming struggle.

'The National Socialist movement will in the future ruthlessly prevent – if necessary by force – all meetings or lectures that are likely to distract the minds of our fellow countrymen.' [13]

Röhm's contribution to the rise of the party was not limited to providing protection and persuasion. As an army officer he had influence with the Bavarian authorities, who turned a blind eye to Nazi violence and the intimidation of their political rivals. They believed that the Nazis would crush the Marxist menace in the region. But within ten years the gangster tactics of Röhm's brownshirts were seen as tarnishing the image of the party and his homosexual affairs were an embarrassment that the leadership was not prepared to tolerate. In 1934 Hitler would order his execution and that of hundreds of the SA leadership in a slaughter known as the Night of the Long Knives. This was Nazi 'politics' in practice.

INFIGHTING

Within months of joining the party Hitler had pressured Drexler into appointing him head of propaganda. Then, as he had planned, he forced the founders to elect him leader in the summer of 1921, after staging a tantrum and threatening to leave if he didn't get his way.

It seems that Hitler had become too auto-cratic for the party's liking and far too ambitious. In a bid to popularize the party beyond Bavaria he had travelled to Berlin in order to negotiate with the north German nationalists. Meanwhile Drexler was considering an alliance with the German Socialist Party, which was based in Nuremberg and led by the sadistic Jew-baiter and pornographer Julius Streicher, editor of *Der Stürmer*. It looked as if the party would split before it had a chance to make an impression. Hitler returned to Munich to learn that his own party was plotting against him and was issuing libellous leaflets attacking his leadership and loyalties.

'A lust for power and personal ambition have caused Herr Adolf Hitler to return to his post after his six weeks' stay in Berlin, of which the purpose has not yet been disclosed. He regards the time as ripe for bringing disunion and schism in our ranks by means of shadowy people behind him and thus further the interests of the Jews and their friends. It grows more and

'Being a Jew is a crime': poster for a special anti-Semitic edition of *Der Stürmer*

more clear that his purpose is simply to use the National Socialist party as a springboard for his own immoral purposes and to seize the leadership in order to force the party on to a different track at the psychological moment… Make no mistake. Hitler is a demagogue.'

A damning indictment indeed, but it was one that Hitler seized upon in order to strengthen his influence in the party. Under threat of legal action the dissenters were forced to climb down

and Drexler was effectively sidelined when he accepted the role of honorary president. Hitler was now acknowledged as absolute leader of the party.

SPREADING THE WORD

As the party's popularity increased it began to hold meetings in larger halls and outdoor venues. The massed banner-wielding ranks of the SA made a memorable impression on the

THE TRUE NATIONAL SOCIALIST [14]

What is the first commandment of every National Socialist?
Love Germany more than anything and your fellow Germans more than yourself!...

What does it mean to be a National Socialist?
To be a National Socialist means nothing but: Fight, Faith, Work, Sacrifice!

What do we National Socialists want for ourselves?
Nothing!...

What ties us National Socialists together in this fight for Germany's freedom within and without our borders?
The awareness of belonging to a community of fate, a community imbued with a spirit of radical innovation, a community whose members shall be companions, one to the other, in good times and in bad.

What is the National Socialist password to freedom?
God helps those who help themselves!...

press and visiting dignitaries with their military discipline and sense of order.

One of the first outsiders to report on the growing movement was Captain Truman Smith, an assistant military attaché at the American Embassy in Berlin. He had been ordered to Munich to evaluate the importance of the party and its new leader. His report, dated November 25, 1922, makes it clear that Hitler was becoming a force to be reckoned with.

'The most active political force in Bavaria at the present time is the National Socialist Labour Party. Less a political party than a popular movement, it must be considered as the Bavarian counterpart to the Italian *fascisti*... It has recently acquired a political influence quite disproportionate to its actual numerical strength...

Adolf Hitler, from the very first, has been the dominating force in the movement, and the personality of this man has undoubtedly been one of the most important factors contributing to its success... His ability to influence a popular assembly is uncanny.'

Before returning to Berlin Captain Smith managed to obtain a private interview with Hitler at his lodgings, which Smith described in his diary as a 'little bare bedroom on the second floor of a run-down house' at 41 Thierschstrasse, a lower-middle-class district. Afterwards he recorded his impressions of the man he considered to be 'a marvellous demagogue'. He wrote, 'Have rarely listened to such a logical and fanatical man.'

'I GIVE YOU MY WORD OF HONOUR, NEVER AS LONG AS I LIVE WILL I MAKE A PUTSCH!'
Adolf Hitler

Within a year Hitler would attempt to fulfil his promise by seizing power in the city by force.

THE BEER HALL PUTSCH

'I give you my word of honour, never as long as I live will I make a Putsch!'

Hitler's assurance to the Bavarian minister of the interior, summer 1923

By November 1923 Hitler was impatient for power. He was no longer a soapbox agitator, but a prominent figure in the radical nationalist movement. He had watched the newsreels of Mussolini's march on Rome in the previous year with awe and was inspired to attempt a similar coup d'état in Germany. His initial idea was to mobilize the disparate anti-republican nationalist forces in Bavaria and with these groups behind him enlist the support of the armed patriotic leagues and the army under Röhm. All would then march on Berlin with Hitler at the head of the column. It was an audacious and absurdly ambitious plan and it was fated to fail.

Part of the problem was that the public now supported the Weimar government, who were in open defiance of the French occupation of the Ruhr and would not look favourably on armed rebellion. But the SA leadership was restless to act because the authorities were threatening to close down the party newspaper and arrest the leaders of the armed groups that Hitler was counting on to join him.

'The day is coming,' he was told by SA

In 1938 Hitler and his henchmen march to commemorate the Munich Putsch of 1923. Seen through their eyes, a disorganized farce had become a glorious victory for the early Nazis

Commander Lieutenant Wilhelm Brueckner, 'when I won't be able to hold the men back. If nothing happens now, they'll run away from us.'

Fearful of being abandoned by his 'troops' Hitler panicked and gave orders for the takeover of the city.

The original plan was to disrupt a military parade on Memorial Day, 4 November and take the visiting dignitaries hostage. These would include Crown Prince Rupprecht and three regional leaders – State Commissioner von Kahr, General Otto von Lossow and Colonel Hans von Seisser, head of the state police. But the plan had to be abandoned when news reached the plotters that armed police had sealed off the route of their attack as a precaution.

An alternative plan was hastily drawn up for the morning of 11 November, Armistice Day. The SA was to storm strategic points in the city while a detachment attempted to force Kahr,

Lossow and Seisser to join the revolution. A date was set but it had to be brought forward when Hitler learned that the three regional leaders were to hold a public meeting at the Bürgerbräukeller in the suburbs of Munich on 8 November. He feared the purpose of the meeting was to proclaim Bavarian independence along with the restoration of the monarchy – so it was now or never.

BLUFF AND BLUNDER

At 8.45 on the evening of 8 November, Hitler led a large detachment of the SA to the Bürgerbräukeller and ordered them to surround it. A machine gun was set up at the entrance and the rear exits were sealed. Hitler burst in, disrupting Kahr's address, while the bewildered crowd sat in silence, unsure of what was happening. They did not have to wait long to find out. Hitler clambered on to a table while brandishing a pistol and fired one shot at the ceiling. Then he jumped down and strode up to the stage. Waving the smoking firearm at a senior police officer he ordered him to step aside – which he did, along with Kahr. This left the stage free for Hitler to address the crowd.

'The National Revolution has begun! This building is occupied by 600 heavily armed men. No one may leave the hall. Unless there is immediate quiet I shall have a machine gun posted in the gallery. The Bavarian and Reich governments have been removed and a provisional national government formed. The barracks of the Reichswehr and the police are occupied. The army and the police are marching on the city under the swastika banner.'

The last part of Hitler's statement was a lie. However, the crowd was intimidated by the presence of the armed SA. But not by Hitler – one witness described him as looking 'ridiculous' in his ill-fitting morning coat. He went on to say, 'When I saw him jump on the table in that ridiculous costume I thought, "The poor little waiter!"'

Some called for the police to fight back. But their appeal fell on deaf ears for the police had secretly been ordered not to resist. A Nazi infiltrator on the force had telephoned their commanding officer earlier that evening and warned them of what was about to take place. Then Hitler herded the three leaders into a backroom at gunpoint and threatened to shoot them there and then if they did not join his new government. Meanwhile Goering was attempting to quell the grumbling crowd in the hall by reminding them that they had nothing to fear and plenty of free beer.

Kahr took a chance and called Hitler's bluff by revealing the former corporal for the posturing fraudster he was. Cornered, Hitler played his trump card. He announced that he had the support of General von Ludendorff, hero of the First World War, and that the general was on his way to ask them to reconsider the offer to join the rebels. In reality, von Ludendorff had been kept in the dark regarding the coup and when he arrived at the hall he was livid to discover his name had been used to endorse such a chaotic enterprise. He was also furious to learn that Hitler intended to declare himself leader of the new regime while he, Ludendorff, would be relegated to commander of the army. But in the old soldier's mind the sword had been unsheathed and could not be returned to its scabbard without dishonour. He believed that he

General von Ludendorff was furious to learn that Hitler had used his name in vain

had little choice but to tell the three hostages that it would be in Germany's interest if they joined the cause. Meanwhile Hitler returned to the hall where the audience was getting restless and informed them that their leaders had agreed to form a new government.

'Tomorrow will find either a National Government in Germany or us dead!'

This declaration was greeted with ecstatic cheers which persuaded the men in the back-room that it might be better to go along with the mob for the moment. It was then that Hitler made a crucial blunder. He left the Bürgerbräukeller to sort out a clash between an SA battalion and a regular army unit at the Engineer's Barracks, leaving General von Ludendorff in charge. The general then released the opposition leaders on the understanding that they would organize their forces in support of the coup. Instead they immediately mobilized the army and the police, who stationed them-selves in the centre of the city to await the rebels.

No-one had thought to cut communications with the outside world, so as soon as word reached Berlin that an armed uprising was under way orders were sent to the Bavarian Army to suppress it before it could spread. State Commissioner Gustav von Kahr even had time to print up and distribute posters around the city, which refuted rumours that he had acceded to the demands of the rebels and denounced them as traitors.

'The deception and perfidy of ambitious comrades have converted a demonstration into a scene of disgusting violence. The declarations extorted from myself, General von Lossow and Colonel Seisser at the point of the revolver are null and void. The National Socialist German Workers Party, as well as the fighting leagues Oberland and Reichskriegsflagge are dissolved.'

THE FINAL BLUFF

Having returned to the beer hall to discover that his revolution was unravelling, Hitler was now in a panic as to what to do next. He couldn't call it off, but without his hostages he had little chance of success. It was Ludendorff who whipped the demoralized demagogue into action. The general shamed Hitler into acting by accusing him of being a defeatist and an armchair revolutionary. The only course open to them, the general assured him, was to attempt another bluff.

Towards noon they marshalled their forces in the garden of the beer keller and marched them down the narrow Residenzstrasse leading to the Odeonsplatz, with Ludendorff at their head. Although it has been stated that there may have been as many as three thousand armed men marching behind Hitler and the general that morning, they did not look as intimidating as they had hoped.

'If you saw one of our squads from 1923 marching by you would ask, "What workhouse did they escape from?"' Hitler later confessed.

Their presence was sufficiently alarming,

'TOMORROW WILL FIND EITHER A NATIONAL GOVERNMENT IN GERMANY OR US DEAD!'

however, to have drawn a detachment of 100 armed police, who awaited them at the end of the narrow street. They were supported by an army unit at the rear. As the rebel force entered the square Hitler pulled his pistol from his pocket and demanded that the police surrender. A moment later a shot rang out – no one knows who fired first – and the police emptied a volley into the advancing column. Sixteen Nazis were killed, while their leaders scattered at the sound of the first shots.

Hitler had linked arms with the man marching next to him and was pulled down when his companion was hit. According to several eyewitnesses, including one of the would-be rebels, Dr Walther Schulz, Hitler 'was the first to get up and turn back'. He escaped in a waiting car only to be arrested some days later while hiding in the attic of a supporter. It was reported that he was 'almost incoherent' with rage.

Hermann Goering, who cut a formidable figure in the party both because of his wide girth and his bulldog ferocity, was seriously wounded but managed to get treated by a local Jewish doctor. He was then smuggled to safety in Austria where his pain was eased with morphine, a drug to which he became addicted. Hess also abandoned his fallen comrades and ran. He eventually found temporary shelter across the border in Austria, but was later arrested. Only Heinrich Himmler escaped unnoticed. He had not been recognized by the authorities when they were rounding up the stragglers, so he was able to slip through the side streets and make his way to the railway station, where he boarded a train for home.

General Ludendorff, the nominal figurehead of the abortive coup, was given safe passage through the police lines, being treated with the respect befitting a befuddled old soldier who had been led astray.

HITLER ON TRIAL

The putsch was a humiliating disaster for the Nazis and a personal blow to Hitler, whose political career appeared to be in tatters. But the trial was to prove a triumph. Hitler had been assured that the judges were sympathetic to the right-wing cause. He would be safe to argue that it was wrong to prosecute him for treason when he was only trying to bring down those who had wrested power from the Kaiser. Taking the stage in the dock before the world's press he gave one

Playing the martyr: Hitler in his surprisingly luxurious cell at Landsberg prison

Hitler's trial, 1924: one of the few remaining photographs of an event that became a propaganda coup

of the most impassioned speeches of his life. For four hours he argued that he was not a traitor, but a counter-revolutionary intent on restoring the nation's honour.

Stunning those who had expected him to deny complicity in the plot, as the Kapp Putsch conspirators had done years before, he freely admitted his involvement. Here was Adolf Hitler the actor, relishing his moment in the spotlight, knowing his every word would be recorded by the assembled reporters.

'I alone bear the responsibility. But I am not a criminal because of that. If today I stand here as a revolutionary, it is as a revolutionary against the revolution. There is no such thing as treason against the traitors of 1918.'

Nor would he deny that his part in the putsch was motivated by personal ambition.

'The man who is born to be a dictator is not compelled. He wills it. He is not driven forward, but drives himself… The man who feels called upon to govern a people has no right to say, "If you want me, summon me, I will cooperate."

No! It is his duty to step forward.'

In closing he turned on the judges.

'It is not you, gentlemen, who will pass judgement on us. You may pronounce us as guilty a thousand times over, but the Goddess of the eternal court of history will smile and tear to tatters the brief of the state prosecutor and the sentence of this court. For she acquits us.'

Under Article 81 of the German Penal Code the judges were obliged to find him guilty for inciting armed rebellion, but they showed where their true sympathies lay by imposing a minimal five-year sentence, knowing that he would serve only a fraction of that. Hitler had lost the case, but had won the admiration of the German nationalists and the publicity had made him a national figure. The nine months he was to spend in Landsberg prison were to prove the most productive of his life.

MEIN KAMPF

Life in Landsberg was the closest thing to luxury Hitler had experienced to date. He was given a comfortable furnished private room with a view of the river Lech and was waited on by both prisoners and guards. Each one considered it an honour to act as his servant. He slept until noon every day and was allowed to abstain from exercise, which he disdained. His reason was that political leaders cannot afford to take part in sport and other frivolous activities in case they are beaten and lose face. A steady stream of visitors brought him gifts and provided a much-needed audience and on his 35th birthday admirers sent fruit, flowers and wine from all over Germany. By the end of the day the 'cell' resembled a 'delicatessen store'.

When the party's business manager Max Amann offered to publish his memoirs Hitler welcomed the opportunity to relieve the tedium. He began to dictate to his faithful servant and secretary Rudolf Hess, who corrected the leader's schoolboy grammar and attempted to shape his rambling, random monologues into something cohesive and concise. It was not easy. Hitler was fired up by the chance to discourse on any topic he chose and once he had found his voice, the words would gush forth in a torrent. It was difficult and exhausting to keep him focused on one subject. But Hess had help from two anti-Semitic journalists, Father Bernhard Staempfle and Josef Czerny of the *Völkischer Beobachter*, both of whom toned down and even edited out some of the more inflammatory passages.

When it was finished, the manuscript was delivered to Amann who was horrified to discover that the inside story of the abortive putsch had been relegated to a few sentences. The remaining 782 pages were devoted to discourses on any subject about which its author believed himself to be an expert. These ranged from comic books to venereal disease, on which Hitler rambled for ten turgid pages. Even the title invited derision. With a stroke of the pen Amann reduced the unwieldy *Four and a Half Years of Struggle Against Lies, Stupidity and Cowardice* to *Mein Kampf* (*My Struggle*). He then insisted on publishing the ponderous tome in two volumes of 400 pages each, but even that did not ensure reasonable sales. In 1925, the first year of publication, it sold fewer than 10,000 copies and thereafter sales declined until 1933.

At that point Hitler became chancellor and every loyal German was required to own a copy. By 1940 6 million copies had been sold in Germany alone, and many more thousands were sold abroad, making its author a millionaire. But it is difficult to believe that more than a few thousand people managed to finish it. This was unfortunate for as William L. Shirer, author of *The Rise and Fall of the Third Reich*, observed, '... the blueprint of the Third Reich, and what is more, of the barbaric New Order which Hitler inflicted on conquered Europe... is set down in all its appalling crudity at great length and in detail between the covers of this revealing book.'

Those who persisted with it learnt of his fanatical devotion to the concept of *Lebensraum* (living space), which permitted strong nations to take territory by force from their weaker neighbours. This theory tied in with its author's *Weltanschauung* (worldview) which stated that life was a struggle for survival and that the strongest need have no compassion or concern for the weak.

They would also have discovered that the failure of the Munich Putsch had convinced Hitler that armed rebellion might succeed in the short term, but it would not win the hearts and

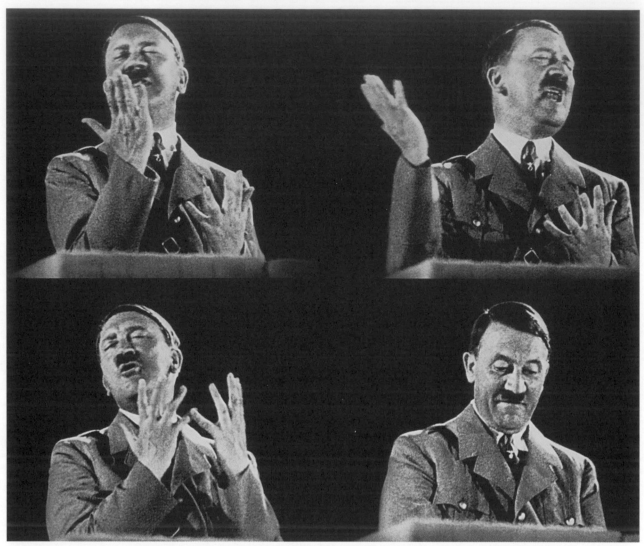

Perfecting the pose: this sequence of photographs illustrates Hitler's increasingly contrived mannerisms up on the podium. Like an actor, he practised the gestures that would move the crowd

minds of the people. Persuasion and propaganda were needed to convert the nation to the Nazi worldview.

'We shall have to hold our noses and enter the Reichstag… If outvoting them takes longer than out-shooting them, at least the results will be guaranteed by their own constitution!... Sooner or later we shall have a majority and after that we shall have Germany.'

REINVENTING HITLER

The reversal in the party's fortunes coincided with a drastic change of image for their leader. The man largely responsible for reinventing Hitler and making him presentable as a politician was Professor Karl Haushofer (1869–1946). The academic had been a regular visitor to Landsberg Prison where he had introduced Hitler to the theories of geopolitics and the concept of *Lebensraum*. These two ideas were crucial to the formation of Hitler's foreign policy, but equally important were the changes the professor made to Hitler's personal image.

Haushofer persuaded his protégé to change his Bavarian *Lederhosen* for a tailored suit or an SA uniform and discard the riding crop which had become his trademark. He then convinced Hitler that he should drink herbal tea after a long speech in order to quench his thirst and clear his head. His customary flagon of strong Bavarian beer might well have an adverse effect on his powers. The professor also offered to train

Hitler in the art of public speaking, which required him to practise a range of gestures that would serve to emphasize his arguments and increase his self-confidence.

IN THE WILDERNESS

Hitler would need all the self-confidence he could muster when he emerged from prison on 20 December 1924. His party had been declared illegal, its newspaper had been closed down by order of the state and Hitler himself was banned from public speaking. There was even talk of deporting him to his native Austria. But little was done to enforce the bans on the Nazis and their newspaper, or to prevent Hitler from speaking to private groups of followers who had remained loyal despite the setbacks.

The main reason why no-one bothered with Hitler at that time was that he was no longer considered a threat. The runaway inflation of the early 1920s had been cured by a newcomer to the republican government, Dr Hjalmar Schacht, and other measures had been implemented to ease the burden on the German economy. For instance, the Dawes Plan had been introduced, which reduced Germany's reparation payments and brought investment from the United States. Security issues had been addressed by the Locarno Treaty and an acceptable compromise had been reached between the Weimar administration and the Allies, which promised to bring Germany into the League of Nations in due course. Taken together, these measures helped ease public anxiety and bolstered the vote for the ruling Social Democrats in the elections that were held that December. The Nazi vote was halved.

While his acolytes hovered around their demoralized leader, urging him to rekindle the faltering flame of the party, Hitler's interest in politics appeared to wane. A new obsession had taken hold of him. Her name was Geli Raubal.

FATAL ATTRACTION

Geli was Hitler's 20-year-old niece, the youngest daughter of Angela, his half-sister. Angela had recently answered Hitler's summons

One of Hitler's rare unguarded moments (with his niece Geli Raubal): 'Uncle Adolf' began to spend more and more time in Geli's company and was jealous when she showed interest in other men

to serve as his housekeeper in his new Alpine retreat Haus Wachenfeld, on the Obersalzberg near Berchtesgaden. Hitler later bought the villa and had it extensively rebuilt, renaming it the Berghof.

At first, 'Uncle Adolf' was merely attentive to the pretty brunette with the peaches and cream complexion and the infectious smile. Then her mother noticed that he was spending more time with her than with his party comrades and that he was intensely jealous whenever she showed interest in other men.

If Angela had any misgivings about the nature of their relationship – the furtive glances and unchaperoned long walks in the country – she kept it to herself. But she must have realized that her daughter was about the same age as her own mother had been when she married and that the age gap between Geli and Adolf was similar to the one that had existed between Klara and Alois. They had also taken to calling each other 'Uncle' and 'Niece' rather than using first names, just as Adolf's parents had done. It was nothing she could object to, but it must have made her uncomfortable nevertheless.

And then there were the frequent and furious rows arising from Geli's ambition to pursue a singing career in Vienna. Whenever they argued his mask of doting docility fell away, revealing a ferocious jealousy which left Geli in tears. He demanded that she put such foolishness aside and assured her that he would furnish her with everything she needed after they moved to Munich. He had just purchased a luxury apartment for them there, using party funds. This seemed to mollify her for the time being and they resumed their walks in the country and trips to the town. She certainly enjoyed his lamb-like loyalty and appreciated his many gifts.

Hitler's official photographer Heinrich Hofmann observed: 'He watched and gloated over her like some servant with a rare and lovely bloom, and to cherish and protect her was his one and only concern.'

A SHAMEFUL SECRET

But over time Geli's happy-go-lucky nature wilted under his domineering personality. And she resented being spied upon by the party police whenever she went out and by the household staff whenever he was away. When pressed, Geli complained to her mother that Hitler's intense attention was stifling and that he wanted to control every aspect of her life, including her choice of clothes and the company she kept.

But Angela suspected that her daughter might be tormented by a more shameful secret. Hitler biographer Konrad Heiden mentions a compromising letter dated 1929 in which Hitler is said to have confessed that he needed Geli to satisfy his masochistic desires.

The letter fell into the hands of the landlord's son, but was then retrieved by Father Staepmfle. Whatever was in the letter was obviously so potentially damaging to the Führer that he was evidently not satisfied with its recovery, for knowledge of its existence cost Staempfle his life during the bloodpurge of 1934.

Other insiders spoke of there being 'something very unusual' about Hitler's relationship with Geli which proved 'unbearable' for her and that she was desperately unhappy because she could not do 'what he wants me to'.[15] Even so, it is thought that her mother remained ignorant of this secret and simply thought Geli wanted to be free of his unrelenting scrutiny.

When confronted by Angela's anxieties Hitler assured her that there was nothing for her to

In public Hitler aligned himself with the heroes of Germany's past, but according to his generals he lacked the qualities of disciplined leadership to exploit his early military success

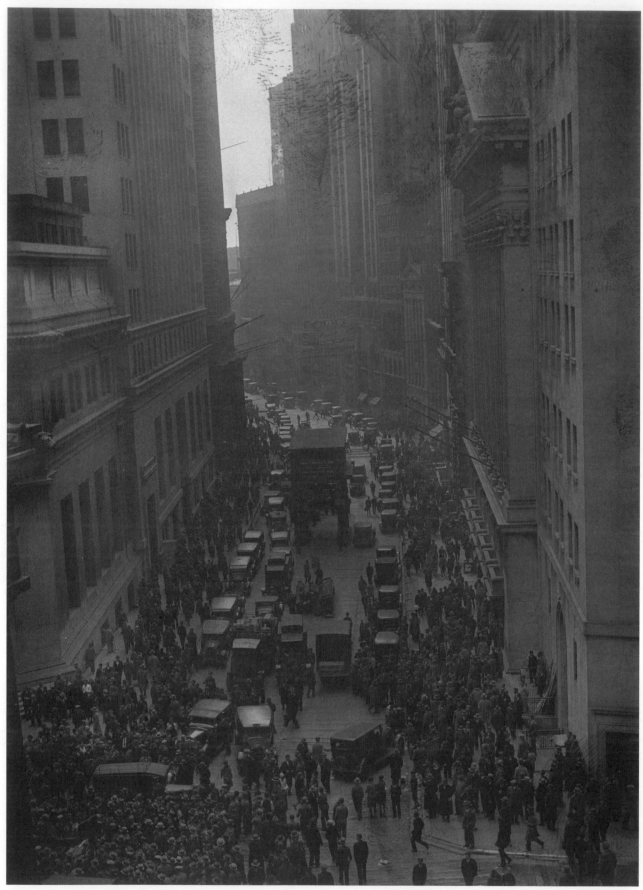

Wall Street four days before the terrible stock market crash of 1929: 'In America only the mobsters turned a profit. In Germany it was the turn of the political gangsters.'

A BRIEF INTERVAL (1924–9)

It could be argued that the Nazis' rise to power was unavoidable given the prevailing conditions in Germany during the Weimar years. The temporary reversal in the nation's misfortunes achieved by Chancellor Gustav Stresemann and his new government after 1923 perhaps only forestalled the inevitable. Stresemann himself was under no illusions that the measures he had taken (which included replacing the Deutsche Mark with a new currency, the Rentenmark, and securing over 25 billion marks in foreign loans) were akin to putting a sticking plaster on an open wound. Germany was ailing and the cure was too awful to contemplate. As he said in 1929

'The economic position is only flourishing on the surface. Germany is in fact dancing on a volcano. If the short term loans are called in [by the American financial institutions] a large section of our economy would collapse.'

Across the Atlantic the artificial high that had been sustained on the profits of bootleg booze and gambling in the financial markets finally burst. The Stock Market Crash of 1929 ushered in the Great Depression. As Stresemann had feared, the American banks immediately called in their loans in a frantic effort to save themselves and in so doing bankrupted countless thriving businesses at home and abroad. Millions were thrown out of work and the West was plunged into darkness and despair. The party they had called 'The Roaring Twenties' was over. The Great Depression had begun. In America only the mobsters turned a profit. In Germany it was the turn of the political gangsters.

worry about, that Geli simply resented the fact that he had forbidden her to pursue an operatic career. This may well be the case, for on the afternoon of 17 September 1931, as he left for a meeting in Nuremberg, Geli was heard to call out to her uncle from an upstairs window.

'So you won't allow me to go to Vienna?'

'No!' he curtly replied.

Next morning Geli was found dead with a bullet lodged in her heart and Hitler's Walther 6.35 mm pistol at her side. She was just 23 years old, the victim of an apparent suicide.

But no suicide note was recovered. However, an unfinished note to a friend in Vienna lay near the body. It ended, 'When I come to Vienna – hopefully very soon – we'll drive together to Semmering an…' It suggests that she might have shot herself after Adolf had reneged on an earlier promise to let her leave. Some historians have speculated that her letter was unfinished because she was interrupted by someone who had been ordered to silence her – probably Himmler. But if this was so, surely the letter would have been destroyed and not left to give that impression.

News of her death brought Hitler scurrying back. His grief almost consumed him. After a week of intense pain Hitler emerged from his self-imposed solitude and declared that under no circumstances was her name to be mentioned in his presence. Then he ordered her bedroom to be preserved as a shrine and forbade anyone to enter but his trusted servant, the matronly Frau Winter. As his grief subsided he commissioned a sculpture and posthumous portraits were painted from photographs. These he kept in his bedroom along with a portrait of his mother, which hung over his bed until his death.

Geli was, he confessed, the only woman he had ever truly loved, but it is evident that he had suffocated her with what his friend Hanfstaengl later called 'his twisted tenderness'.

CHAPTER FIVE
STORMING TO POWER

REACHING THE MASSES

Between 1924 and 1928 the Nazis made a serious tactical blunder in trying to appeal to the industrial workers, who remained loyal to the Communists and the Social Democrats. This strategy also isolated the party from the middle classes, who thought that the Nazis were now only interested in speaking for the working classes. As a consequence their share of the vote declined. In the 1924 national elections they won 32 seats in the Reichstag, half as many as the Communist Party and about a third of the number of seats won by the Nationalists and the Social Democrats, who won 95 and 100 seats respectively. At the end of that year a second election was held after which the two leading parties gained more seats at the expense of the Communists, who dropped from 62 to 45 while the Nazi Party lost 18 seats. Four years later in May 1928 their share of seats fell to an all-time low of just 12.

Thirty-one million Germans had exercised their democratic right at the ballot box, but fewer than one million had cast their vote for the Nazis. Political commentators dismissed them as a spent force. The American correspondent William L. Shirer observed, 'One scarcely heard of Hitler or the Nazis except as butts of jokes.' But the Great Depression altered all that. In just over a year, unemployment tripled to almost four and a half million. It was *Schadenfreude* writ large. The nation's misfortune was the Nazi's miraculous stroke of luck.

Hitler ordered the activists to target the rural communities, where the farmers had been badly hit by falling prices and the craftsmen were threatened with extinction by mass production. The Nazis also canvassed the smaller towns. Here the shopkeepers were struggling for

Street fighting men: Nazi troops proudly bear a Death's Head banner at Braunschweig in 1931

survival against the chain stores and the middle-class workers had seen the value of their savings wiped out.

As the party's newspaper reported in May 1928: 'The election results from the rural areas in particular have proved that with a smaller expenditure of energy, money and time better results can be achieved there than in the big cities. In smaller towns mass meetings with good speakers are events and are often talked about for weeks, while in the big cities the effects of meetings with even three or four thousand people soon disappear.'

Goebbels proved to be a master of manipulation and was not averse to fighting dirty if it earned extra votes. His philosophy was simple – if you repeat a lie often enough people will begin to believe it. Hitler too, believed that to indoctrinate the masses it was necessary to hammer home the same message again and again until all resistance had crumbled and even the most intransigent citizens had been converted.

A typical Nazi leaflet from April 1932 read, 'Middle-class citizens! Retailers! Craftsmen! Tradesmen!

'A new blow aimed at your ruin is being prepared and carried out in Hanover!

'The present system enables the giant concern WOOLWORTH (America) to build a new vampire business in the centre of the city. Put an end to this system. Defend yourself middle-class citizen! Join the mighty organization that alone is in a position to conquer your arch-enemies. Fight with us in the Section for Craftsmen and Retail Traders within the great freedom movement of Adolf Hitler.'

It is clear from the above example that the Nazis drew much support by appealing directly to the voters' self-interest (despite their claim to the contrary) and that they exploited middle-class fears and prejudices regarding big business and Jewish-owned corporations. But it is generally overlooked that the core of Hitler's supporters in the 1920s and early 1930s were not politically motivated but were ordinary citizens who desperately wanted to believe in his promise to provide them with their basic needs – work and bread. Those who were aware of the activities of the SA reassured themselves that once in power Hitler would bring the

> **'WHOEVER CONQUERS THE STREETS, CONQUERS THE MASSES AND WHOEVER CONQUERS THE MASSES, CONQUERS THE STATE.'**
>
> *Nazi maxim*

extremists into line. They did not realize that the Nazi Party was extremist by definition.

Hitler seized the opportunity to spread his message by radio, which guaranteed an audience of millions, and he made exhausting tours of the country in the belief that a personal appearance by the leader would leave a more lasting impression. In the 1932 presidential elections he crossed the country by plane which enabled him to speak in several cities every day. Posters were designed to appeal to particular groups of voters such as mothers, workers, farmers and shopkeepers. Even the timing of the poster campaign was calculated for maximum impact.

Goebbels wrote to local activists in his capacity as organizer of the 1932 elections.

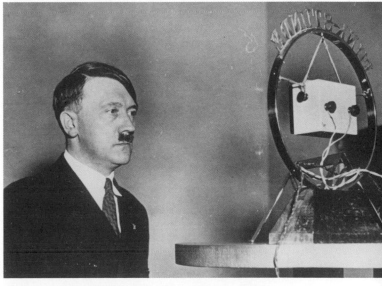

Hitler making his first radio address to the German people on 1 February, 1933

Nazi Party Appeal to Voters, Presidential Election 1932 [16]

LEAD GERMANY TO FREEDOM

Hitler is the password of all who believe in Germany's resurrection.

Hitler is the last hope of those who were deprived of everything; of farm and home, of savings, of employment, survival and who have but one possession left: their faith in a just Germany which will once again grant to its citizens honour, freedom and bread.

Hitler is the word of deliverance for millions for they are in despair and see only in this name a path to new life and creativity.

Hitler was bequeathed the legacy of the 2 million dead comrades of the World War who died not for the present system of the gradual destruction of our nation, but for Germany's future.

Hitler is the man of the people hated by the enemy because he understands the people and fights for the people.

Hitler is the furious will of Germany's youth, which, in the midst of a tired generation is fighting for new forms and neither can, nor will, abandon its faith in a better German future. Hence Hitler is the password and the flaming signal of all who wish for a German future.

All of them on March 13 will call out to the men of the old system who promised them freedom and dignity and delivered stones and words instead: We have known enough of you, now you are to know us!

Hitler will win because the people want his victory!

'The Hitler poster depicts a fascinating Hitler head on a completely black background. In accordance with the Führer's wish, this poster is to be put up only during the final days [of the campaign]. Since experience shows that during the final days there is a variety of coloured posters, this poster with its completely black background will contrast with all the others and will produce a tremendous effect on the masses.'

A year later the party merged with the German Nationalist Party, which swelled its membership and fighting fund considerably as well as giving it a veneer of respectability. The leader of the GNP, Alfred Hugenberg, was a wealthy and influential newspaper owner who had also acquired the UFA film studios and cinema chain. He immediately put his newspapers and newsreels at Hitler's disposal. No one was laughing now.

CHANCELLOR HITLER

Contrary to popular myth, the Nazis did not seize power by force, nor were they elected. In the last national elections before Hitler became Chancellor of Germany their share of the vote had actually fallen from 37 per cent to 33 per cent, giving them fewer than 200 seats in the Reichstag, only a third of the total. They gained power because Hitler was handed the chancellorship by Hindenburg in the hope that it would end the political in-fighting that had brought the Weimar government to its knees.

For Germany, the repercussions of the Wall Street Crash of October 1929 were more than financial. The fissures in Germany's already precarious coalition were widened until it finally crumbled when the Nazis and the Communists refused to prop up the tottering structure. President Hindenburg was then forced to take personal charge.

From 1930 onwards Germany was ruled by the almost senile old soldier, who took advice from an ambitious army officer, Kurt von Schleicher. Von Schleicher manoeuvred Hindenburg into appointing chancellors who would rubber-stamp measures benefiting the army. The first of these was Heinrich Brüning and the second was Franz von Papen, who

1933: Hitler greets Hindenberg with outstretched hand and a deferential bow, but the haughty aristocrat was outfoxed by the 'upstart Austrian corporal' when he handed over the reins of power

March 1933: defying the downpour, Nazi storm troopers ride in triumph through the Brandenburg Gate for the newsreel cameras and receive a stiff-armed salute from the hand-picked crowd

succeeded Brüning in May 1932. In December of that year von Papen was replaced by von Schleicher. This angered von Papen who offered Hitler a place in his government if Hitler would agree to help him unseat Schleicher. But first von Papen would have to get the support of Hindenburg, who was known to distrust Hitler whom he called 'the upstart Austrian corporal'.

Earlier that year, in August and again in November, Hitler had demanded the chancellorship only to be briskly rebuffed by von Hindenburg. The minutes of that first meeting between Hindenburg and Hitler on August 13 reveal that the old soldier was not so senile as

to be unaware of the threat that Hitler and his party posed to the democracy and to personal freedom.

'Considering the importance of the National Socialist movement [Hitler] would have to demand the full and complete leadership of government for himself and his party. President Hindenburg thereupon stated emphatically that he had to respond to this demand with a clear and determined "No". He could not, before God, his conscience and the fatherland bear all responsibility of entrusting all Governmental authority to a single party, a party moreover, which held to such a one-sided attitude toward people with convictions different to theirs…'

But von Papen persisted and finally managed to persuade the ailing president that he could restrain Hitler in two ways. First of all by limiting the number of Nazi ministers in the government and then by insisting that Hitler be forced to work with his political rivals in the cabinet.

Hindenburg relented and sacked Schleicher. On 30 January 1933 Adolf Hitler was appointed Chancellor of Germany.

DEMOCRACY INTO DICTATORSHIP

The Nazis celebrated their succession with a mass torchlight parade of brown-shirted storm troopers through the streets of Berlin. Now no one could be in any doubt that Germany was under the heel of a fascist military dictatorship. But even as Hitler waved to the adoring crowds from the balcony of the Chancellery he was acutely aware that millions of Germans were still out of step with the movement. The dead wood of the democratic institutions would have to be cut away leaving only the sturdy stock of the party. So the new government's first proclamation was aimed at reassuring the people of their conservative credentials.

'The new national government will consider its first and supreme duty to restore our nation's unity of will and spirit. It will safeguard and defend the foundation on which the strength of our nation rests. It will firmly protect Christianity, the basis of our entire morality, it will safeguard the family… It wants to base the education of Germany's youth on a reverence for our great past, on pride in our old traditions. It will thus declare war on spiritual, political and cultural nihilism… the government will once again make national discipline our guide.'

THE REICHSTAG FIRE

Even as the echo of the jackbooted storm troopers died away down the Unter den Linden Hitler knew that his hold on power could still be challenged by the Communists, who shared his contempt for democracy. At the last election 63 per cent of the voters had rejected the Nazi call to arms and no one in the leadership could afford to rule out the possibility of a counter-revolution financed by the Soviets. The Nazis were in a minority in parliament and President Hindenburg had the power to dismiss Hitler at any time if he chose to do so.

Hitler would not be pacified until his grip on government was secure. What was needed was a specific threat to the new regime. No one is certain who dreamt up the idea of setting fire to the Reichstag and blaming it on the Communists

When the Reichstag went up in flames, Hitler had the perfect pretext for seizing power

– some historians claim it was Goering – but it was a brilliant and despicable demonstration of Nazi politics in practice.

On February 27 the Reichstag building in Berlin was gutted by fire and a lone Communist, Marinus van der Lubbe, was hastily tried and executed for the crime. Van der Lubbe was an obvious fall guy who was chosen by the Nazis because he was feeble-minded and would not speak in his own defence. The imaginary plot gave the regime the excuse it needed to imprison 4,000 Communist Party officials and call fresh elections to endorse their policies.

On February 28 Hitler successfully demanded that Hindenburg pass an emergency decree which banned freedom of speech and political meetings by the opposition and also authorized the state to search private homes. But although this severely restricted the opposition parties' ability to campaign, the Nazis did not receive the overwhelming endorsement they had confidently predicted. They secured 288 seats, but it was still well short of a majority. More draconian measures would be needed. A series of laws were drawn up with the intention of tightening the government's stranglehold on democracy.

First of all there was The Enabling Act. Passed by the Nazis on March 24, it gave Hitler the right to make laws without needing the approval of parliament. Then in May further decrees were approved which banned the Communist Party. The following month, it was the turn of the Social Democrats. In July the regime pressured the Vatican into closing down the Catholic Centre Party in Germany in exchange for a guarantee that the church would be permitted to operate without state interference.

Also in July the second major law, the Law

Against the Formation of Parties, was passed by the regime. It forbade anyone from forming a new political party, under the threat of imprisonment. The new year saw the abolition of the state parliaments that represented the regions. Party and state were now one and the same.

The third significant measure was the Law Concerning the Head of the German State, which was enacted after the death of President von Hindenburg on 1 August 1934. This law combined the offices of president and chancellor so that Hitler became absolute ruler of Germany.

Before the old man could be buried Hitler abolished the office of president and assumed the role of Head of State. His first act was to

Reign of terror: auxiliary policemen (SA thugs drafted into the police) arrest members of the Communist Party as the battle between left and right for German cities intensifies in 1933

demand that all members of the armed forces swear a personal oath of loyalty to their Führer, a shrewd and cynical move that ensured that they could not disobey an order from Hitler without being disloyal to the Fatherland.

With Hindenburg's passing the old Imperial Germany was laid to rest. Hitler was now Führer of a new empire. He boasted that it would last for a thousand years. In fact, Hitler's Third Reich lasted for barely 12 years.

NIGHT OF THE LONG KNIVES

If any one had harboured hopes that the Nazis might be brought to heel once they were in government, they were cruelly disillusioned by the events of 30 June 1934. It was on that day that the Hitler gang slaughtered their own in a bloodbath that could have left no one in doubt as to what the regime stood for – nor to what lengths it was prepared to go to in order to crush opposition and cover up its past 'mistakes'.

For some time Hitler and Röhm had been in disagreement over the future role of the SA. Hitler was indebted to his old comrade, who had been instrumental in his rise to power. But Röhm's increasingly angry exchanges in the Reichstag with General von Blomberg, Hitler's first minister of defence, had become both an embarrassment and a threat to the Führer's authority. Time and again Röhm had demanded that the SA be officially acknowledged as the 'people's revolutionary army'. He also urged that the regular army be purged of the Prussian officer elite and the rank and file be assimilated into the SA.

It was not an unreasonable request from Röhm's point of view. With a total of 3 million men at his command he led one of the largest armed forces in Europe, one that outnumbered the regular army by four to one. But the Prussian officers were horrified at the prospect of a bunch of hoodlums and sexual deviants, as they thought, tainting the honourable tradition of their regiments. Rumours of Röhm's homosexual activities, and those of his inner circle, were circulating with increasing frequency and it was only a matter of time before they became public knowledge. That was something that would discredit the entire movement.

As General von Brauchitsch observed: '... rearmament was too serious and difficult a business to permit the participation of speculators, drunkards and homosexuals.'

Hitler was also disturbed to learn that his financial backers shared the army's concerns. For instance, Gustav Krupp, who had personally pledged 3 million Reichsmarks to party funds, confirmed the Führer's fears that the SA were now seen as Röhm's private army and therefore as a threat to the state. As the owner of the largest iron and steel works, Krupp was crucial to Germany's rearmament programme.

News that the SA were arming themselves with heavy calibre machine guns in open defiance of the Versailles Treaty could not be allowed to go unchallenged. Hitler had no close personal friends and would turn on a trusted comrade or colleague for the least infraction. Nevertheless, he made repeated efforts to persuade Röhm that the time had come to disband the 'old fighters' and accept that the revolution was over.

But Röhm was stiff-necked and not a man to be reasoned with. The turning point came on 11 April 1934, during naval exercises in East Prussia attended by General von Blomberg and the commanders-in-chief of the armed forces, General von Fritsch and Admiral Raeder. Hitler knew he had to secure their support if he was to cement his hold on power, especially once the ailing Hindenburg was out of the picture. So while they dined aboard a cruiser, the *Deutschland*, en route to Koenigsberg [now Kaliningrad] he outlined his plans to build a fleet that would be the envy of the world. He also described his vision of a new Wehrmacht that would be equipped with tanks and heavy artillery in defiance of the hated treaty, regardless of the expense.

In return he pressed them for an assurance that when Hindenburg died they would name him as his successor and order every member of the armed forces to swear an oath of allegiance to their Führer as the Supreme Commander. If

'HAVEN'T I WORKED HARD ALL MY LIFE FOR THIS LAND AND GIVEN HITLER ALL I HAD. WHERE WOULD HE BE WITHOUT ME? HITLER HAD BETTER LOOK OUT – THE GERMAN REVOLUTION IS ONLY BEGINNING...'

Ernst Röhm to Kurt Ludecke, June 1933[17]

Paying their respects: Adolf Hitler and Ernst Röhm proceed to the Cenotaph at Nuremberg in September 1933. Less than a year later, Röhm was executed after Hitler deemed him superfluous

28 June 1934: Hitler at the wedding of Josef Terboven to Ilse Stahl, once Goebbels' mistress

Fritsch and Raeder would place their faith in him, he would curb the SA and guarantee that the regular forces would be the sole bearers of arms in the new Reich. Had he not already implemented, at the cost of billions of marks, a massive public works programme that would revitalize the economy and restore the nation's pride? How could they say no to such an offer? Having secured their support Hitler was now free to act against the enemy within.

SETTLING OLD SCORES

When word reached Hitler that Röhm was planning a putsch – a fantasy hatched by Himmler and Goering to spur their leader into

action – Hitler gave orders for his immediate arrest and execution together with the senior SA leadership. It was the order Himmler and Goering had been waiting for – a chance to settle old scores with the Führer's blessing and without having to account for their actions.

On the night of 30 June 1934 150 members of the SA leadership in Berlin were rounded up and summarily shot by black-shirted members of Himmler's personal bodyguard, the SS, and by Goering's special police squads. Many died with a last 'Heil Hitler' on their lips, believing that it was Himmler and Goering who had ordered their death and not the Führer.

That same night a column of black limousines pulled up in front of the Hanslbauer Hotel in Wiessee near Munich where the SA leader was on vacation. Hitler, his face set in grim determination, watched as dozens of bewildered SA men were dragged from their beds and immediately executed. Then Hitler entered Röhm's room and spewed forth a torrent of abuse and accusations. Following his departure, Röhm was removed to Stadelheim Prison where he was presented with a loaded pistol and told to accept a soldier's death.

'If I am to be killed, let Adolf do it himself,' he replied, defiant to the end.

Two SA guards then entered the cell and shot their leader in the back of the head.

No one knows for certain exactly how many men met their deaths in what became known as the Night of the Long Knives. In his speech to the Reichstag on July 13, in which he sought to justify the executions, Hitler admitted to 77 deaths. But in a postwar trial some of the perpetrators admitted that 'more than 1,000' had been murdered. This figure included Gustav von Kahr who had helped to foil the

Beer Hall Putsch and Father Staempfle who had edited *Mein Kampf* and was said to be privy to the true circumstances of Geli Raubals' death. Kahr was hacked to death with pickaxes and dumped in a swamp near Dachau; Staempfle was found face down in a forest outside Munich, his neck broken and three bullets lodged in his chest.

Other victims included two army officers, General von Bredow and General von Schleicher (Hitler's predecessor as chancellor) plus Gregor Strasser, who had openly defied Hitler's authority in the early days of the party. Dozens more were shot at random as the SS and SA assassination squads ransacked the offices and homes of party officials whom they suspected of disloyalty or other indiscretions. The former Prussian premier Franz von Papen escaped with his life, but his secretary was killed and other associates died later in prison. Erich Klausener, head of Catholic Action, was gunned down in his office and his entire staff were bundled off to a concentration camp.

Germany was now in a permanent state of emergency in which civil liberties had been suspended indefinitely. Under such circumstances, few took comfort in Hitler's assurance that there would be no other revolution in Germany for a thousand years.

The next morning Germans read the news with grim resignation and realised that the New Order meant that justice would now be dispensed without even the pretence of a trial. Imprisonment and death were to be meted out at the whim of Reichsführer Himmler, Goering and the rest of the Hitler gang, all of whom acted as if they were the new feudal lords. In that respect they were right – Germany had descended into a new Dark Age.

AFTERMATH

The implications of the army's complicity in the massacre were profound. They had not only supplied transportation for the prisoners but also weapons for their executioners. In praising Hitler for his swift and decisive action against the 'traitors' in the days following the killings General von Blomberg had aligned the army with the dictatorship. Any thoughts that the generals might have entertained regarding the enforced removal of Hitler were now out of the question for Blomberg had voiced his approval of the Führer's actions. From this moment on the credibility of the officer corps was fatally compromised.

30 June 1934: the body of Ernst Röhm seems to be giving one last salute following execution

CHAPTER SIX

THE THOUSAND-YEAR REICH

HITLER'S ARCHITECT

Six weeks after Hitler became chancellor an obscure but promising young architect received a telephone call summoning him to Berlin. Albert Speer, then just 27 years old, accepted the invitation without hesitation and drove through the night from his home in Mannheim, arriving weary but eager at party headquarters. He was met by District Organization Leader Hanke, the official who had called him to the capital, and was told to report to the 'Herr Doctor', who wished to inspect an imposing 19th century building he had chosen for his new ministry.

Dr Goebbels greeted Speer with uncharacteristic cordiality and wasted no time in ushering him into an official car. Together they drove to the Wilhelmsplatz where a large crowd had gathered hoping for a sight of the Führer whose Chancellery was directly opposite. Speer surveyed the expectant faces of the strangers who now shared a common bond – hope for the future and faith in their Führer. As the car turned into the spacious courtyard of the ministry he had a sense that a new epoch was beginning and that he was taking his place at the centre of it all.

Speer had joined the party at a comparatively late stage, in 1931, and had been dismayed to discover that the local party members were petty bureaucrats of a 'low personal and intellectual level'. He could not imagine them governing the nation. But it would become clear to him over the following weeks that it was the force of Hitler's personality that empowered such nonentities. And it was their desire to please him that oiled the wheels of the regime.

As they toured the building Goebbels made it clear that no expense was to be spared in renovating the offices and great halls in the

Building the future: Albert Speer outlines his plans for a new classic German architecture

grand imperial style that befitted his status. In common with all of the regime's building projects no budget had been agreed and no plans had been approved, so Speer had a totally free hand. Even so, when he prepared his sketches he opted for modest classical lines in keeping with the original architect's intentions. To his dismay these embellishments did not meet with Goebbels' approval. He found them 'insufficiently impressive' and commissioned a Munich firm to remodel the building in what Speer later referred to as 'ocean-liner style'.

However, Speer was given a second chance shortly afterwards when Goebbels asked him to refurbish his private residence, a commission the young architect rashly promised to complete in just two months. Using three teams of labourers working around the clock Speer managed to bring the job in before the deadline, a feat which brought him to the attention of Hitler, as he had hoped. The other members of the Führer's inner circle were initially suspicious of the newcomer and resented having to share their leader's attention and favours.

Whatever they all thought, it was perhaps inevitable that Hitler, himself a failed architect, would take to Speer and entrust him with the realization of his imperialist fantasies. It gave the Führer great pleasure to have someone around him with whom he could discuss his plans for rebuilding Berlin and Linz, as the new capital of Austria.

GERMANIA
Berlin was to be a city of impressive monuments and public buildings. Everything was to be built on a scale that would dwarf the structures of the ancient world. Running through the centre of the capital would be a broad avenue 400 feet (122 metres) wide and three miles (5 kilometres) long. There would be a 400-foot-high (122 metres) triumphal arch at one end, on which would be inscribed the names of the German war dead, and a domed conference hall at the other. Detailed plans were drawn up and models were constructed to scale, but the war intervened and 'Germania', as Berlin was to be renamed, was never built.

Instead, Speer was inveigled into redesigning the residences of top party officials. This gave him the opportunity to observe the leadership at close hand and appreciate how suspicious they were of each other. Goebbels was known to

loathe Goering, Ribbentrop and Bormann, while Ribbentrop despised everyone in the administration – and the feeling was reciprocated. Goering mistrusted Ribbentrop, Goebbels, Bormann and Speer, although he commissioned Speer to redesign his home only months after it had been refurbished at considerable expense. And all because Hitler had complained that it resembled a mausoleum. It would appear that the leading Nazis all adhered to the belief that one should keep one's friends close but one's enemies closer.

A CATHEDRAL OF LIGHT
With each commission Speer's reputation increased, but his most significant contribution to the regime was designing the setting for the annual Nuremberg Rallies. When he first arrived in Berlin he noticed a sketch for the staging of a party meeting at Berlin's Tempelhof Airfield and immediately claimed he could do better. Taking inspiration from the theatre and ancient Rome he designed a large stage, at the back of which rose three huge swastika banners, each one taller than a ten-storey building. The banners were illuminated by powerful searchlights.

Later on, when he came to design the setting for the Nuremberg Rallies, he went one better. He commandeered 130 anti-aircraft searchlights which he placed at 40-foot (12-metre) intervals, each of them pointing upwards to create the illusion of gigantic pillars rising into the vaultless sky. In this 'cathedral of light' Hitler assumed a messianic stature in the eyes of his fanatical followers. The event became a ritual celebration of military might and the power of the collective will.

If Speer had any pangs of conscience, he kept them to himself, for the only unforgivable sin in

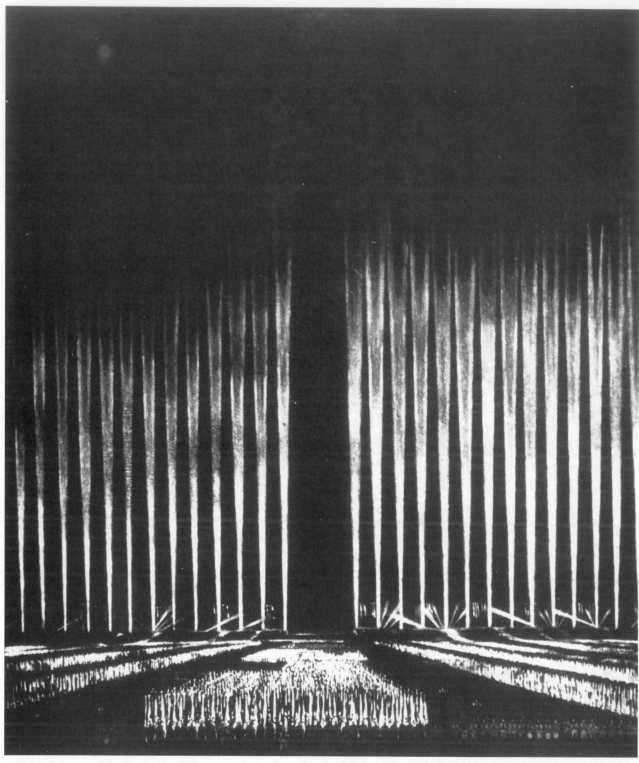

Albert Speer's 'Cathedral of Light', the crowning moment of the 1937 Nuremberg Rally. A hundred and thirty anti-aircraft searchlights pointed skywards, creating the illusion of gigantic pillars

the Third Reich was disloyalty to the Führer. All other indiscretions were overlooked.

CENTRE OF EMPIRE

Hitler frequently boasted that his empire would last for a thousand years, so he required buildings that would reflect the regime's historic significance. In 1938 he entrusted Speer with the design of a new Chancellery in Berlin. It was to be erected on the site of the old Imperial Chancellery and would extend along an entire city block on Voss Strasse. It was conceived on a scale that invited comparison with the monuments of the ancient world and was designed to intimidate visiting dignitaries. Hitler hoped they would be left in awe of the 'power and grandeur of the German Reich'. The entrance was certainly impressive. The courtyard, which was over 200 feet (61 metres) long, led to a short flight of steps. These were flanked by 42-foot-high (13 metres) neoclassical columns and two bronze statues designed by Hitler's favourite sculptor, Arno Brecker.

Inside, the floor and walls of the 150-foot-long (46 metres) Mosaic Hall were constructed from red marble. This was inlaid with eagles of grey marble and ornamented with gold decorations that recalled the palaces of the Roman emperors. Hitler had even adopted the Imperial Eagle as an emblem. Gold eagles were perched over every entrance, wreaths holding swastikas gripped in their claws.

In order to reach the Führer's office, visitors passed through the Great Marble Gallery which at 480 feet (146 metres) long was twice the length of the Hall of Mirrors at Versailles. It was lined with priceless tapestries on permanent loan from the capital's museum. Hitler's office was suitably imposing and tastefully furnished, the one telling feature being a half-drawn sword motif inlaid into the top of his desk.

'When diplomats see that they'll learn to shiver and shake,' he said.

Beyond Hitler's private office lay the Cabinet Room, along the centre of which ran a long conference table ringed with two dozen Empire chairs. All were decorated with the eagle and the swastika. Ironically Hitler never held a cabinet meeting there so ministers had to content themselves with a brief visit in order to see their names embossed in gold on the writing pad at their place of honour.

The Long Hall in the Third Reich's new chancellery, a building which carried echoes of Versailles and was similarly designed to cow and intimidate all those who entered

More than 4,500 labourers were hired to construct the new Chancellery and thousands more were employed across the country in the production of the luxurious fixtures and fittings. These included huge mahogany doors 17 feet (5 metres) high, gold wall lights and gold plaques depicting Plato's four virtues: Wisdom, Fortitude, Temperance and Justice. Their presence made no impression on Hitler who boasted, 'You would hardly believe what a power a small mind acquires over the people around him when he is able to show himself in such imposing circumstances.'

It was one of the few really insightful remarks that he was to make in his lifetime, but the irony was clearly lost on him.

BORMANN, THE BROWN EMINENCE

Hitler's indolence and disdain for paperwork meant that no one in the new administration knew what their duties were and everyone was being continually undermined by their colleagues. Hitler, whose orders were invariably vague and contradictory, summed up his attitude to the chaos he created by comparing himself to a gardener who looks over the fence from time to time to watch his plants struggling for the light. Matters were not helped by the structure of Hitler's administration, a Kafkaesque labyrinth of bureaucrats with each district ruled by a *Gauleiter* (district leader). These officials could block or delay orders if they did not like the office that had issued them.

As Hitler's press secretary, Otto Dietrich, once remarked, 'Hitler created in the political leadership of Germany the greatest confusion that has ever existed in a civilized state.'

Perhaps he was unconsciously defying his father whose sense of order and respect for bureaucracy was one of Hitler's pet hates.

Fortunately for the Führer, he was surrounded by sycophants ever eager to carry out his directives and record his every thought for posterity. The most faithful of these underlings was Martin Bormann, whose dogged devotion and unquestioning subservience exceeded even that of his superior, Rudolf Hess.

July 1944: Hitler and senior officers six days after the attempt on his life by Claus von Stauffenberg at the Wolf's Lair. On their orders, the cruellest possible retribution was being exacted

Bormann was a short stocky man with pronounced arched shoulders and a thin reedy voice that precluded him from public speaking. Instead he remained in the shadows, an anonymous but constant presence. In fact, he guarded his access to the Führer so zealously that he refused to take a holiday for fear that someone else would wheedle their way into Hitler's confidence. As a consequence he was reviled by the entire Nazi hierarchy, who named him the Brown Eminence in reference to the colour of his uniform and his ever-lurking presence. His official duties were to take care of the Führer's personal finances, which he performed with an obsessive zeal. It was Bormann who had the idea of demanding a royalty from the German postal service for every stamp that bore Hitler's portrait. This amounted to millions of marks within a few years. And it was Bormann who administered a secret slush fund from contributions made by the rich industrialists who had grown fat on lucrative rearmament contracts. The fund amounted to over 100 million marks in the first year alone.

But instead of lining his own pockets, as many officials might have been tempted to do in such a lax and self-serving regime, Bormann curried favour with his Führer by lavishing millions of marks on renovating the Berghof, Hitler's Alpine retreat at Berchtesgaden. The original modestly sized lodge was extended into a multi-storey chalet, whose lower floors were hewn out of the mountainside to accommodate living quarters, kitchens and store rooms. But the most spectacular feature was the immense picture window, which offered a spectacular view of the Austrian Alps. Even though the mountain-top residence was practically inaccessible it was surrounded by barbed wire and heavily guarded at all times. In the mid-1930s Bormann found the funds to construct a tea house on the summit, known as the Eagle's Nest, which was connected by a private lift shaft that had to be dug out of the granite. That feature alone was said to have cost up to 30 million marks, giving rise to the gibe that Bormann was the only person who had created a reverse gold rush by ploughing money into a mountain.

Despite being an unprepossessing figure, Bormann had a colourful history. After joining the party in 1927 at the age of 26 he became involved with a Nazi murder squad and was sent to prison for one year for his participation in the killing of his former elementary school teacher. But after marrying the daughter of a high-ranking Nazi official he was able to persuade Hess to appoint him as his deputy. He then shrewdly made himself available for the tedious paperwork that he knew Hess abhorred.

A born bureaucrat, he knew that the real power of an administration was to be found in restricting access to the decision-maker. So he trailed after Hitler with a pad and pencil from the moment the leader woke up at midday until the early hours. He recorded every order, every passing remark. No comment or query was considered too trivial for Bormann to write down. By this means he ingratiated himself with Hitler, who came to rely on him to draft his casual remarks into official orders and to summarize the issues requiring his attention. Hitler paid Bormann the highest compliment he could imagine when he remarked, 'With him I deal in ten minutes with a pile of documents for which with another man I should need hours.'

Bormann even appeared to share the leader's liking for vegetarian meals, but behind Hitler's back he would sneak off to his own quarters and gorge himself on pork chops and schnitzel.

CHAPTER SEVEN

HITLER – BEHIND CLOSED DOORS

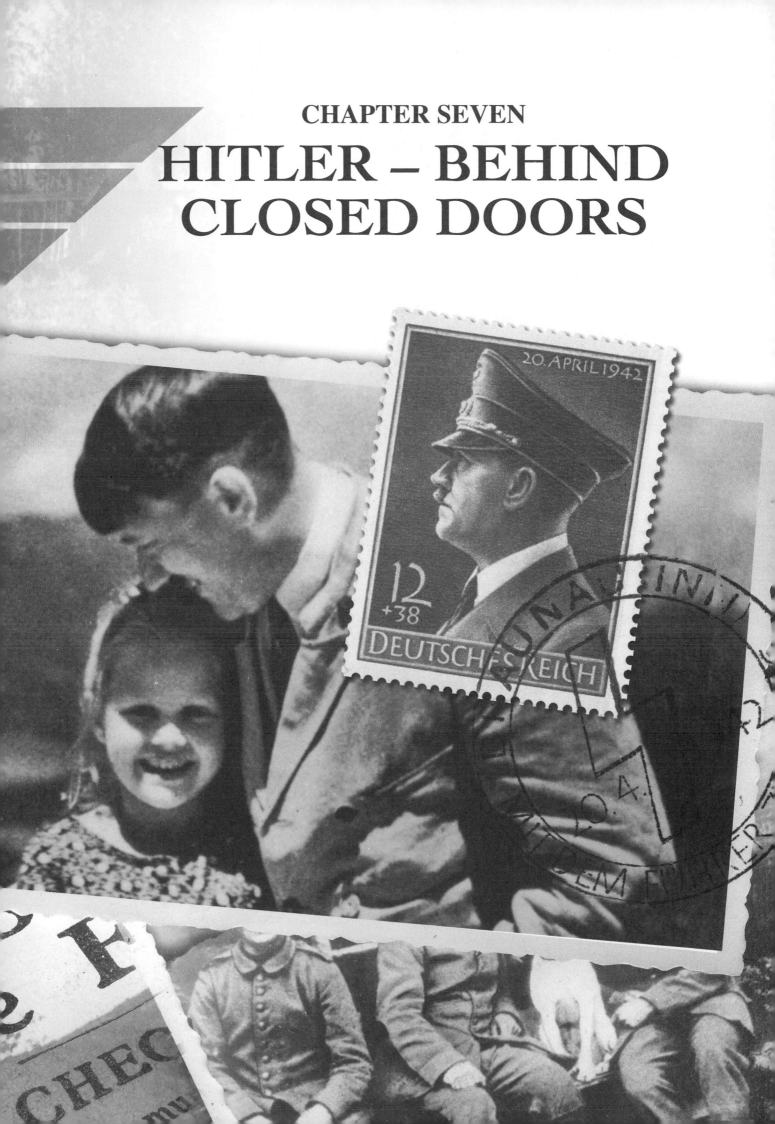

TEA WITH A TYRANT

Between the wars foreign dignitaries flocked to Berchtesgaden to take tea with the leader who had worked an 'economic miracle' by regenerating Germany. They were invariably shocked to find an indolent, ungracious host who slept in until midday, indulged in aimless monologues and ate copious quantities of cream cakes and chocolates. Moreover, he whiled away his evenings watching movies as if he were a retired gentleman with no pressing matters of state to attend to.

When he did consent to meet with ministers and his inner circle, many important decisions were decided intuitively, or without the consideration his visitors would have afforded them. He acted like a Ruritanian prince who was preoccupied with pomp and pageantry rather than the realities of modern diplomacy. Although he was often credited at the time with astute political insight and shrewd statesmanship, his early successes were the result of a combination of bullying and bluff. What he demonstrated was little more than pure animal cunning. He was able to sense the weakness of his prey and his enemies' lack of resolve to protect an ailing ally.

But for a time he fooled the great and the good. King Edward Vll and his new American bride Wallace Simpson were among the visitors to the Eagle's Nest on the Obersalzburg. The former British prime minister David Lloyd-George was another visitor. He was so enthusiastic in his praise that his comments had to be toned down before they were published in the *Daily Express*.

'I have now seen the famous German leader and also the great change he has effected… There is for the first time since the war a general sense of security. The people are more cheerful… It is a happier Germany. One man has accomplished this miracle. He is a born leader of men. A magnetic, dynamic personality with a single-minded purpose, a resolute will and a dauntless heart… The old trust him. The young idolize him. It is not the admiration accorded to a popular Leader. It is the worship of a national hero who has saved his country from utter despondency and degradation… not a word of criticism or of disapproval have I heard of Hitler.

'What Hitler said at Nuremberg is true. The Germans will resist to the death every invader of their own country, but they have no longer the desire themselves to invade any other land.' [19]

HITLER IN PRIVATE

For all the talk of his personal magnetism and powers of oratory, the abiding impression of Hitler, derived from those who knew him and attended upon him on a daily basis, was that of a shallow, gauche and insufferable bourgeois. He delighted in shocking his guests and companions. For example, he was in the habit of telling women that their make-up had been manufactured from human fat, sewage or kitchen waste. When meat was served, the

> 'I SHALL BECOME THE GREATEST MAN IN HISTORY. I HAVE TO GAIN IMMORTALITY EVEN IF THE WHOLE GERMAN NATION PERISHES IN THE PROCESS.'
> *Adolf Hitler* [18]

Top of the world: Adolf Hitler and guests share the mountain sunshine on the Berghof terrace

avowed vegetarian would point out its resemblance to a roast baby, or describe the scene inside the slaughterhouse in graphic detail. Yet he fretted over his tea parties like a middle-class *Hausfrau*.

In order to avoid being reminded of his intellectual shortcomings Hitler deliberately surrounded himself with those he considered his inferiors. If they were physically deformed, all the better. His personal adjutants, Bruckner and Burgdorf, were of low intellectual ability, as were his three SS aides Fegelein, Günsche and Rattenhuber. Rudolf Hess was another example. He must surely have been the most intellectually challenged deputy leader of a modern European country. His ill-fated flight to Scotland in May 1940 in pursuit of peace was naive in the extreme and quite possibly suggestive of insanity.

Physically, too, they were an odd assortment. Hitler's chauffeur was so short that he had to have blocks placed under his seat so that he could see over the steering wheel. This perverse policy could also be seen in the appointment of the club-footed Goebbels, the one-armed party business manager Max Amann and a stone-deaf assistant press secretary.

After the assassination of Ernest Röhm, Hitler then appointed the one-eyed Victor Lutze as his successor, while Robert Ley, head of the Labour Front, was burdened with a speech defect which amused Hitler. He took a perverse delight in giving him as many public-speaking engagements as he could organize.

But not all of Hitler's appointments were intended to amuse. Many of the Nazi elite were sadists, sexual degenerates, drug addicts, alcoholics, pornographers and petty criminals,

Cult of the personality: before the war, vast crowds used to come to the Obersalzberg, where Hitler and other Nazis had their mountain retreats, to catch a glimpse of the Führer or to touch his hand

all of whom would have been jailed had they not scrambled to the top of the heap in Hitler's criminal administration. Hermann Goering, for example, was considered by his Führer to be 'the greatest genius in aviation history', but it is said that he spent most of the Second World War in a narcotic haze. Meanwhile, his foreign minister, Joachim von Ribbentrop, had as lamentable a grasp of world affairs as a fourth form schoolboy. Hitler's childlike glee at causing confusion and his cavalier attitude to state affairs led him to duplicate various duties, so that his ministers and officials would be too busy arguing among themselves to pose a threat to his leadership. It was also said that Hitler considered anyone who had recently had a holiday abroad as an expert in foreign affairs.

But as with all tyrants and dictators, Hitler sowed the seeds of his own destruction by surrounding himself with sycophants and insisting on his own infallibility. Had he been willing to delegate authority to more able men and listen to the advice of the more capable officers in the armed forces the Third Reich might have lasted far longer. But as his press secretary remarked, 'Instead of drawing to himself men of high character, rich experience and breadth of vision, he gave such persons a wide berth and made sure they had no chance to influence him… [He] permitted no other gods beside himself.'

THE MAD MESSIAH

In his exhaustive and penetrating study of Hitler's personality, *The Psychopathic God*, the historian Robert G L Waite argues that the Nazi state could be seen as the creation of a 'perverse child's fantasies'. He goes on to draw parallels between Hitler's New Order and the savage society created by the shipwrecked schoolboys in William Golding's novel, *Lord of the Flies*. Both Hitler and the central character in Golding's book are textbook psychopathic personalities who will typically begin their criminal career as the neighbourhood bully. They will dominate the weak and 'dare' their followers to commit minor offences in order to tighten their hold over them. Tiring of this they may seek notoriety in adulthood as the leader of a cult or sect because they seek adoration, self-aggrandisement and the vindication of their hatred against the world.

Such men are contemptuous of the weak. They celebrate mindless destruction and they enjoy gratuitous cruelty. One of their ploys is to stage elaborate rituals with music, marching and the veneration of ancient symbols in order to create the illusion that their subordinates belong to a community with a respected tradition. As a result of this indoctrination their followers will be less likely to question their leader's orders when asked to humiliate, intimidate or even murder those who don't conform. Devoid of conscience, their leader will blame his victims for having brought their fate upon themselves, while his collaborators will absolve themselves of responsibility, feeling neither compassion nor remorse. If called to account they will say that they had been conditioned to follow orders.

BEHIND THE MASK

It is revealing that Hitler styled himself 'the greatest actor in Europe' – and with some justification, for he was a master of manipulation and deceit. He used his innate gift for mimicry to deceive his enemies into believing that he was sincere and that his promises could be relied upon. This he achieved by a combination of calculation and conviction, because he was not merely playing a role but living it to the full.

But he was also capable of resorting to melodrama or faking one of his infamous rages if he thought it would achieve the desired effect. During a confrontation with Hjalmar Schacht, the German minister of finance in the Weimar administration, Hitler managed to bring tears to his eyes as he successfully pleaded with Schacht to remain in office. But the moment the minister had left the room Hitler turned on his associates and gave vent to his true feelings. The German Secretary for Foreign Affairs witnessed another persuasive performance on 23 August 1939 when Hitler impressed the British ambassador Sir Neville Henderson.

'Only after Henderson had left the room did I realize that Hitler's performance was premeditated and acted.'

Hitler styled himself 'the greatest actor in Europe': he was always aware of being centre-stage

Father of the nation: Hitler hugs a suitably chosen little girl for the camera

He would also rehearse a conversation at length in private with his deputy Rudolf Hess before meeting a foreign dignitary or diplomat, trying out various voices until he found the appropriate tone.

Hitler was a consummate actor. He fulfilled the role that was expected of him, so that everyone was taken in, but when he had departed the world stage for good not even his closest companions could convey the qualities that had captivated them.

His architect and armaments minister, Albert Speer, who considered himself the only friend Hitler ever had, if indeed he had ever been capable of friendship, confessed, 'In retrospect, I am completely uncertain when and where he was ever really himself, his image not distorted by playacting.'

His personal pilot, Hans Baur, recalled that it was only in the company of children, whom he did not have to impress, that he showed anything

resembling genuine human feeling. And yet he ordered the murder and enslavement of hundreds of thousands of children from afar and was responsible for many more becoming homeless orphans.

As the historian Robert Waite remarked, 'Hitler did not possess the qualities and attributes that he desired or that others wanted to see in him, he only gave the illusion of possessing them.'

The belief that Hitler was a borderline personality seems borne out by his capacity to have been all things to all men and yet remain indefinable. Peter Kleist, who served as assistant to Nazi foreign minister Joachim von Ribbentrop, notes in his memoirs that Hitler's face always fascinated him because of the '... multiplicity of expressions it contained. It was as though it were composed of a whole series of individual elements without adding up to a single total… A photographer, by selecting only a single moment out of context, could show only one aspect, thereby giving a false impression of the duplicity or multiplicity of being which lay behind it...' [20]

INFALLIBILITY

Examples of Hitler's inability to deal with disagreement and disappointment are revealing. He was once described by a British diplomat as acting 'like a spoiled sulky child' when anyone dared to disagree with him, or the topic of conversation was not to his liking. And his rages were legendary. They were invariably triggered by an insignificant or perceived slight rather than a major setback to his plans. Military defeats would sober him, but if a servant dared to bring him the wrong kind of mineral water or it was suggested that he was whistling a tune incorrectly he would have a tantrum on the spot regardless of who might be watching. He would beat his fists, scream incoherently and even spread himself martyr-like against a wall as if crucified – strategies no doubt originally developed in order to obtain his mother's attention. On one occasion he responded to a secretary's criticism of his whistling by assuring her that he had not deviated from the melody – it was the composer who was at fault!

A childhood acquaintance recalled that he was incapable of passing over something with a smile while an official of the foreign office remembered, 'Concerning people, Hitler's judgments were usually bitter and derogatory.

Qualities such as forbearance, humour and self-irony were completely foreign to him.'

The only time he laughed was at the expense of others. According to his architect and armaments minister Albert Speer, 'He seemed to enjoy destroying the reputation and self-respect of even his close associates and faithful comrades.'

That might have been because his overbearing arrogance and contempt for others was tempered by a tendency to self-pity, which led him to seek reassurance and sympathy for all that he imagined he had suffered and sacrificed on behalf of the German people. Hitler constantly whined about his fear of being

Geographically Nuremberg was at the centre of the Third Reich and the rallies held there, which up to a quarter of a million people attended, were designed to show Germany's new military might

forgotten in order that his acolytes would be stung into reassuring him that he was a great man and destined to be remembered for centuries to come.

It was his morbid obsession with death and the obsessive fear of his own mortality that drove him to commission the building of an inordinate number of monuments to martyrs of the movement. He also planned monumental imperialist buildings with a view to what they would look like as ruins after a thousand years had passed, when the Reich had passed into history.

The death motif was as dominant a theme in the Third Reich as in many of Wagner's operas. Nazi rallies were staged as if they were scenes from *Götterdämmerung*, with theatrical lighting and massed uniformed ranks of SS troops in the role of the Teutonic knights, all scored to Wagner's music. The object was to set the scene and stir the German soul. Significantly, the Nazis staged commemorations to fallen heroes more effectively than any other events in their busy calendar.

INFLEXIBILITY

Hitler was also rigid in his routines and habits. As his press chief noted with exasperation, 'He remained perpetually in the same company, among the same faces in the same atmosphere and, I may also say, in the same state of monotony and boredom, producing eternally the same speeches and declarations.'

Speer too remarked on how shallow Hitler appeared in private, a mere shadow of his fiery public persona. Recalling the long repetitious monologues with which Hitler entertained his guests and cronies, Speer recalled, 'The repertory remained the same. He neither extended nor deepened it, scarcely ever enriched it by new approaches. He did not even try to cover up the frequent repetitions. I cannot say I found his remarks very impressive.'

Hitler spoke incessantly on his favourite subjects: the early struggle of the party, his knowledge of history, his taste in architecture, his favourite film actresses and the private indiscretions of party officials who were not, of course, present. Contributions from guests were not required, only muted agreement with everything their host had said. Meal times were not a social event but an opportunity for a collective audience with the Führer.

But this was a side ordinary citizens did not see. As the absolute ruler of Germany, Hitler was effectively deified in the eyes of millions of his adoring followers. He assumed a mystique that was comparable to that of the Roman emperors or the Egyptian pharaohs.

Goering summed up the German people's fascination with their Führer in a rare article published in 1934.

'There is probably nobody else right now who attracts the general interest as much as the Führer. And yet there is nobody whose qualities are as difficult to describe as are those of Adolf Hitler… there is no single quality or characteristic of his which, to our eyes, he does not possess to the highest perfection... the Führer is infallible… What now is the secret of his powerful influence over his followers?... there is something mystical, unsayable, almost incomprehensible about this man. And the person who does not intuitively sense that will never comprehend it, for we love Adolf Hitler, because we believe, with a faith that is deep and unshakable, that he was sent to us by God to save Germany.' [21]

Hitler had a particular place in the hearts and minds of German women. Here, a party member watches rapt during one of his speeches. She is wearing Nazi insignia and 'the mother's cross'

CHAPTER EIGHT

INSIDE
THE REICH

SPRINGTIME FOR HITLER

Drop by drop the conscience of a nation was being lulled into submission as if an anaesthetic were being administered. But few complained, at least not in public. Life was good. In the first year of Hitler's chancellorship unemployment had been reduced by a third from 6 million to just under 4 million. This was thanks to a massive public works programme, costing 18 billion marks, that guaranteed work for the hundreds of thousands of members of the German Labour Front under Dr Robert Ley. Private firms received massive subsidies if they contributed to the construction of the new motorway system which saw 4,350 miles (7,000 kilometres) of concrete criss-crossing the country. There were also massive new municipal buildings to be erected in Berlin and other administrative centres, including a new Reich Chancellery for the Führer and a complex of ministries on an imposing scale. Several were personally sketched by the Führer who was finally realizing his adolescent ambitions.

In the following year a further million found work and the reduction increased year on year until by 1939 only 302,000 able-bodied Germans were officially unemployed, just 0.5 per cent of the total workforce. For this reason few grumbled at the loss of the unions although they were now forbidden to demand higher wages, shorter hours or improved conditions. Strike action could not be taken under any circumstances. Workers were even prohibited from changing their jobs without permission. Performance-related pay was introduced which benefited younger workers, but proved detrimental to the living of older, less able men and women. Enforced longer hours led to a marked increase in absenteeism. Progress had its price.

The unemployment figures were also deceptive. Conscription was introduced in 1935, which meant that hundreds of thousands of young men were forced into the army, and so did not appear in the statistics. By 1939 one and a half million men were in uniform and so were no longer unemployed.

In rural areas farmers were receiving huge subsidies to produce less food. They were actively discouraged from being productive in order to keep prices artificially high, while in the industrial regions factories were working at full capacity to meet the targets of the rearmament programme. The cost to the nation was 26 billion marks by 1938.

Hitler took the credit for this prosperity, but in fact the German economy improved as a consequence of the global recovery. The Depression had ended and confidence in the major financial institutions had been restored. Even the great road construction programme with which Hitler is credited was actually instigated by the Weimar government at the end of the 1920s. It is a little-known fact that in 1927 the republic was spending more on new roads than the Nazis did in 1934.

> 'WE HAVE PUT A STOP TO THE IDEA THAT IT IS A PART OF EVERYBODY'S CIVIL RIGHTS TO SAY WHATEVER HE PLEASES.'
>
> *Adolf Hitler, 22 February 1942* [22]

The German Games, Nuremberg 1938: under Hitler it was the prime duty of every German citizen to serve the state and, if necessary, lay down his life for the Fatherland

Even the nation's youth was kept busy with healthy outdoor activities that combined physical training with being indoctrinated with Nazi ideology.

HITLER YOUTH

Membership of the Hitler Youth, which had been founded in 1926, was made compulsory for boys from the age of 6 and girls from the age of 10 by a law passed in 1939, which stated, 'It is on youth that the future of the German nation depends. Hence it is necessary to prepare the entire German youth for its coming duties... all of Germany's youth is to be educated physically, mentally and morally in the spirit of National Socialism, to serve the nation and the racial community.'

Before then parents were encouraged to enrol their children in the party organization. Because other youth groups had been banned in 1933,

and church youth groups were abolished three years later, they had little choice but to comply. Those who resisted could be dismissed from their jobs, fined or even imprisoned.

Boys were required to join the *Pimpfen* (Little Fellows) from the age of 6 until the age of 10, at which point they would enrol in the *Jungvolk* (Young Folk) until they were 14. Then they would move up into the *Hitlerjugend* (Hitler Youth), which would train them for military service at the age of 18.

Girls joined the *Jungmädel* (Young Girls) organization at the age of 10. When they reached the age of 14 they moved on to the *Bund Deutscher Mädchen* or *Mädel* (the German Girls' League) until the age of 18.

In 1932, when the youth movement was in its infancy, there were 108,000 members. That rose to nearly five and a half million by 1936 and it reached its peak in 1939 when the total membership of all youth organizations reached 8 million. This ensured that every young person under conscription age was duly indoctrinated with the Nazi programme.

Any concerned parent who was not infected with the fever of National Socialism must have realized that the nation's children were being conditioned to be obedient servants of the state and then infused with Nazi propaganda and cynically prepared for war.

'Himmler is training young men who will

State-sponsored activities: Germany's children were indoctrinated from an early age

make the world tremble,' Hitler remarked.

It was the Grimm Brothers' fairy tale of the Pied Piper brought to life. The majority of boys were happy to be part of the national youth movement and wore their uniforms with pride. They responded eagerly to its ideals of comradeship, loyalty and honour and the promise of sporting contests and camping in the countryside. There they would learn map reading, shooting, signalling and the mystical significance of the runic symbols. For many it was an adventure, a chance to belong. Merit badges could be earned for newly acquired skills and individuals could test their capacity for self-discipline and physical endurance.

But not everyone shared their enthusiasm. A few complained that the military-style discipline was oppressive. Every activity was preceded by repetitive drilling overseen by 12-year-old boys who clearly enjoyed shouting orders at their 10-year-old subordinates. Some relished the authority and the unquestioning obedience they were able to command. They enjoyed the right to punish those who didn't do as they were told. Offenders were given extra drill and latrine cleaning duties.

The youth movement motto was 'Youth must be led by Youth', but in practice it meant that bullies could torment those they disliked. Once indoctrinated with Aryan ideology they would be taught that it was their duty to 'monitor' their parents, their teachers and other adults. They were also instructed to report any incidents or remarks that could be considered acts of disloyalty to the state. The idea was that they were little Hitlers in the making.

The regime's policy was made explicit by Dr Robert Ley, leader of the Nazi Labour Front.

'Our state... does not let a man go free from

the cradle to the grave. We start our work when the child is three. As soon as it begins to think a little flag is put into its hand. Then comes school, the Hitler Youth, the Storm Troopers and military training. We don't let a single soul go, and when all that is done, there is the Labour Front which takes possession of them when they are grown up and does not let them go until they die, whether they like it or not.'

STRENGTH THROUGH JOY

The German Labour Front promoted a programme of leisure activities and social events for workers known as *Kraft durch Freude* (Strength Through Joy) which was intended to keep them happy and productive. Concerts, theatre visits, holidays and educational courses were provided at affordable prices for those who would not otherwise have been able to afford them. But in practice it was still the better paid workers and the management who managed to secure places on the more desirable outings, such as cruises to Scandinavia and Spain. One branch of the organization, known as the 'Beauty of Work' department, sponsored the building of leisure facilities and canteens in factories and other places of employment. However, workers resented the fact that they were expected to construct the facilities in their leisure time and at their own expense.

Ley incurred more resentment by promising every worker a car of their own provided they paid for it in instalments. The beetle-shaped

Political leapfrog: 1936 and the Strength Through Joy movement is in full swing

Volkswagen (People's Car) was said to have been designed by the Führer himself. He laid the foundation stone for the factory in 1938, amid much ballyhoo. But a year later the factory had been turned over to the production of munitions and the cars were never delivered to the workers who had paid for them.

'THE MISSION OF WOMEN IS TO BE BEAUTIFUL AND TO BRING CHILDREN INTO THE WORLD.'
Joseph Goebbels 1929

THE ROLE OF WOMEN IN THE REICH

Women were seen as nothing more than ornaments in Hitler's world. During the Third Reich they were declared ineligible for jury service because, in Hitler's opinion, they were incapable of logical thinking or objective reasoning.

He told the wife of SA leader Franz von Pfeffer, 'A woman must be a cute, cuddly, naive

Der Bund Deutscher Mädel in der Hitler Jugend (The League of German Girls in the Hitler Youth): girls danced together as they were groomed for their future roles as wives, mothers and homemakers

little thing – tender, sweet and stupid.'

His own choice of female companion, the colourless Eva Braun, certainly fitted that description.

The role of women in the Third Reich was summed up by the party slogan *Kinder, Kirche, Küche* (Children, Church, Cooking). Although the Nazi elite chose slender beauties for their mistresses, the party ideal was a matronly wide-hipped woman with no interests outside the home. It was said that the pram was 'the tank of the home front'.

The Nazis feared that the strength of the German population was being threatened by generations of interbreeding with 'inferior races' and that if the trend continued they were likely to be outnumbered by the Slavs. In an effort to counter this situation, the regime encouraged women to leave full-time work so

that they could marry and raise children. Interest-free marriage loans were offered, which would be reduced by a quarter on the birth of each child. Productive mothers were awarded medals in recognition of their loyalty and sacrifice. Those who did not take the hint were actively discouraged from pursuing a career. Places for females on further education courses were drastically reduced in order to limit their options and many professional women were forced out of their jobs. On top of all that, birth control clinics were banned and anti-abortion laws were strictly enforced.

If any branch of science were to be specifically linked with the Nazi Party it would be the specious practice of eugenics, which involved selective breeding programmes aimed at achieving racial 'purification'. In 1936 the Lebensborn child breeding centres were estab-

Scrubbing up with the best of them: Lebensborn was a weird experiment in selective breeding

lished. Racially approved women were paired with SS men in the expectation that they would produce pure Aryan offspring. In parallel with this the Nazis instigated a programme of euthanasia to weed out 'non-productive' citizens so that they did not pass on their 'defects' to their offspring.

EUTHANASIA

In 1933 the Law for the Prevention of Hereditarily Diseased Offspring made sterilization compulsory for the physically disabled, the blind, the deaf and anyone suffering from epilepsy or depression. Even chronic alcoholics were included.

Then in 1935 the Law for the Protection of the Hereditary Health of the German People was passed which forbade people with hereditary or infectious diseases from marrying and producing 'sick and asocial offspring' which would become a 'burden on the community'.

Within four years 200,000 compulsory sterilizations had been performed and a parallel programme for euthanasia was being planned with chilling German efficiency. Gerda

Bernhardt's mentally disabled brother Manfred was one of 5,000 children whose lives were taken by Nazi physicians in the early years of the regime.

Gerda remembers, 'Manfred was a lovely boy, but he could only say "Mama" and "Papa"… He only learnt to walk very late too. He always liked to be busy. If my mother said, "Bring some coal up from the cellar," he wanted to do it over and over again.

'My father was in favour of putting him in some sort of children's hospital and then Aplerbeck came up as they had a big farm there and the boy might be kept occupied.'

Aplerbeck had been designated a 'Special Children's Unit', where the staff decided which patients should live and which would be too much trouble to care for and so should be put to death by lethal injection.

Gerda recalls the last time she saw her brother alive. 'They brought the boy into the waiting room. There was an orderly there when I was leaving. The boy stood at the window and I waved and waved and he waved too. That was the last time I saw him.'

At the time there was no official policy of euthanasia and no law authorizing it, only a *Führerstaat* (directive). Doctors were simply acting on instructions from their superiors who knew that Hitler had casually sanctioned the practice in a letter to his personal physician. That was enough to seal the fate of thousands who were deemed 'undesirable' or unworthy of life. Patients such as Manfred Bernhardt were given overdoses of luminal or morphine and their deaths were ascribed to common ailments in order that the suspicions of the families were not raised (prior to this the method had been starvation). The records of the institution at

Aplerbeck show that Manfred Bernhardt died of measles. In the same week 11 other healthy children passed away prematurely.

SUSPICIONS

But not everyone accepted the official explanation. One family was informed that their loved one had died from an infected appendix but unknown to the institution the patient's appendix had been removed ten years earlier. Similar errors aroused the suspicions of dozens of other families who took their concerns to their priests, knowing that they would not be listened to by the police.

In September 1940 a Protestant clergyman, Pastor Braune, wrote to the Ministry of Justice in order to voice his concerns about the systematic starvation of patients in the church-funded mental homes that were under his supervision.

'Visits to the institutions in Saxony plainly show that the mortality rate is being increased by withholding food... Since the patients cannot possibly survive on that, they are made to take a drug (paraldehyde) which renders them apathetic. Oral and written reports make it movingly clear how the patients time and again call out, "Hunger, hunger". Employees and nurses who cannot bear this any more occasionally use their private means to still some of the hunger. But the result is beyond question. Hundreds have died a quick death in the last few months as a result of these measures.

'NATIONAL SOCIALIST AND CHRISTIAN CONCEPTS ARE IRRECONCILABLE.'

Martin Bormann, July 1941

'Nor are just those patients involved here who are absolutely beyond feeling. On the contrary, these are patients who know quite well what is happening and are watching how many funerals are taking place each day. One report describes the mortal fear of a patient who had an exact presentiment of the fate that is to meet him and his fellow sufferers.'

It was not until August 1941 that Hitler ordered an end to the programme of euthanasia in answer to a well-publicized and public protest by a leading cleric, Bishop Galen of Munster, who had lodged an official protest with the district attorney and the police.

'... lists are being made up in the hospitals and nursing homes of Westphalia of those patients who, as so called "unproductive citizens" are to be moved and soon thereafter killed...

'It probably is to protect the men, who with premeditation kill those poor, sick people, members of our families, that the patients selected for death are moved from near their homes to a distant institution. Some illness is then given as the cause of death. Since the body is cremated immediately, neither the family nor the criminal investigation department can discover whether there really was such an illness and what the cause of death was.

'I have been assured, however, that neither in the Ministry of the Interior nor in the Office of the Reich Leader of Physicians, Dr Conti, is there much effort to hide the fact that premeditated killings of large numbers of the mentally

Worshippers of false gods: Bishop Ludwig Müller with fellow Nazis on the steps of the Castle Church at Wittenberg where Martin Luther once posted his 95 theses against the selling of indulgences

ill have already taken place and that more are planned for the future.'[23]

A DISSENTING VOICE

Few dared to speak out publicly against the regime, but certain members of the clergy, both Protestant and Catholic, criticized the Nazis from the pulpit when it became clear that they intended to supplant Christianity with a new pagan religion. The Christian cross was to be replaced with the swastika and pictures of saints were to be removed from all chapels, churches and cathedrals. Finally, the Bible was to be replaced by *Mein Kampf* and a sword was to be placed on the left of the altar.

In March 1935 Pastor Martin Niemöller of Berlin published an appeal to the congregations of Prussia, warning against this new idolatory.

'We see our people threatened with a mortal danger. The danger is that of a new religion.'

Niemöller, a former submarine commander in the First World War, had initially welcomed the advent of the Nazis. But then he had become swiftly disillusioned by their plans for a state-controlled Reich Church and by the rabidly anti-Christian sentiments expressed by Alfred Rosenberg and other members of Hitler's inner circle. In his bitter condemnation of the regime, Niemöller reminded his fellow Christians that the new religion would be a rebellion against the first commandment, which stated that they were to worship only one God. The worship of blood and race, nationality, honour and freedom constituted new idols, not ideals.

Faith in an 'eternal Germany', he argued, was threatening to replace faith in the eternal heavenly kingdom of Christ and this 'false faith' was an expression of the Antichrist.

115

It was therefore the duty of the Church to resist the secularization of its customs and the de-Christianization of its holy days. The mission of the church was to protect its members from indoctrination into a 'new myth' that was at odds with Christian beliefs.

Niemöller's clerical status did not save him from the wrath of the regime. After he had ignored repeated threats and warnings he was arrested in July 1937 and sent to Sachsenhausen concentration camp and then to Dachau, where he remained for seven years until he was liberated by the Allies. More than 1,000 priests and laymen were arrested in the wake of Niemöller's protest. Eight hundred of them were members of

the Confessional Church that he had founded in response to the pro-Nazi German Christian movement.

With the more principled and vocal pastors removed from the pulpit the remainder reluctantly gave their blessing to the regime. The Nazis did not pursue their plan for a 'National Reich Church', but they ensured that every aspect of religious life was draped in the swastika and given a distinctive military cast. There were Nazi weddings, Nazi baptisms and of course Nazi funerals.

GENOCIDE AND THE JEWS

German Jews did not disappear overnight. They were robbed of their rights and deprived of their livelihoods through a steady and systematic programme of laws. The intention was to isolate them from German society until 'the Final Solution' to the Jewish problem could be implemented. These laws were made public in radio news bulletins, in the weekly cinema newsreels and in the newspapers, so the German people were well aware of what was taking place.

The random harassment of Jews by the SA in the early years of the Nazi regime became explicit party policy in April 1933, when Hitler ordered the boycott of Jewish shops and businesses. Even the aging von Hindenburg knew what was going on. He voiced his disapproval in a letter dated 4 April 1933.

'Dear Mr Chancellor,
In recent days a whole number of cases were reported to me in which judges, lawyers and justice officials who are wounded war veterans and whose conduct of office has been flawless, were forcibly retired and are to be dismissed because of their Jewish descent.

For me personally... this sort of treatment of

Zur Gründung der deutschen Staatskirche

Das Kreuz war noch nicht schwer genug

Nothing was sacred to the Nazis: they produced posters to promote a new German State Church

Jewish officials wounded in the war is quite intolerable.

... If they were worthy of fighting and bleeding for Germany, they must be considered worthy of continuing to serve the Fatherland in their professions.'

With characteristic deviousness Hitler replied that these measures were merely part of a 'cleansing process' that was intended to 'restore the healthy and natural balance' between Germans and Jews in certain professions. He went on to say that it was necessary to purge the system of an 'alien body' which was corrupting it from within.

LEGALIZED PERSECUTION

On April 7 the Law for the Restoration of a Professional Civil Service legalized the dismissal of all Jews from the civil service and public office. In the following month books by Jewish authors were publicly burned in Berlin. More than one reporter was prompted to remind his readers that a hundred years earlier the German romantic poet Heine had warned, 'Where one burns books, there one eventually burns people.'

In September Jews were banned from all cultural activities and in October all Jewish journalists were dismissed from their jobs without compensation. By 1934 Jewish students were forbidden to sit examinations for professional qualifications and in May 1935 all Jews were expelled from the armed forces. That September the infamous Nuremberg Laws deprived German Jews of their citizenship and the Law for the Protection of German Blood and German Honour prohibited both marriage and sexual relations between Jews and Gentiles.

As Heine warned, 'Where one burns books, there one eventually burns people.'

A series of laws that drove the Jews out of the medical, teaching and legal professions followed in 1936. Jewish doctors were only permitted to treat other Jews, Jewish lawyers were restricted to advising and acting for Jewish clients and Jewish teachers could only have private pupils who were also Jews. Both Jewish teachers and Jewish children were excluded from German schools.

Jews were also banned from public places such as parks, restaurants, cinemas and shops. However, during the 1936 Olympic Games all street signs banning Jews from the centre of Berlin were removed for fear of drawing international criticism. But it was only a matter of time before the legalized persecution of the Jews erupted into open violence and attracted the attention of the world's press.

KRISTALLNACHT

On 9 November 1938 a nationwide pogrom known as *Kristallnacht* (the night of broken glass) saw nearly 200 synagogues burned to the ground, while 7,000 Jewish-owned businesses were destroyed and numerous Jewish cemeteries were desecrated. Thirty thousand Jews were arrested and imprisoned in concentration camps, 2,000 of whom were murdered during that week. The violence had been instigated by the Nazi leadership who later stated that it had been a spontaneous reaction by outraged German citizens. It was claimed that the assassination of a German diplomat by a Jewish extremist had provoked the populace.

Berlin housewife, Emmi Bonhoeffer, has no

Shattered illusions: after Kristallnacht the Jews' days in Germany were numbered

patience with those who denied that they knew what was occurring. 'Of course in '38, when the synagogues were burning, everybody knew what was going on. I remember my brother in law told me that he went to his office by train the morning after Kristallnacht and between the stations of Zarienplatz and Zoological Gardens there was a Jewish synagogue on fire and he murmured, "That's a shame on our culture." Right away a gentleman sitting opposite him turned his lapel and showed his party badge and produced his papers showing he was Gestapo. My brother in law had to show his papers and give his address and was ordered to come to the party office next morning at 9 o'clock. He was questioned and had to explain what he had meant by that remark. He tried to talk himself out of it but his punishment was that he had to arrange and distribute the ration cards for the area at the beginning of every month. And he did this for seven years until the end of the war. The family had to arrange the cards for each category of the population, workers, children, etc. but he was not permitted to have a helper. He had to go alone. That was how they broke the back of the people.'[24]

When Emmi learned of what was taking place in the concentration camps she told her neighbours, who said they didn't want to hear such horror stories. It was too much to believe. Such things were created by foreign radio. When Emmi's husband heard what she had been saying he warned her that she was putting her family in the gravest danger. He reminded her that a dictatorship is like a snake – if you attack the tail it will simply turn and bite you. You have to strike the head.

But taking action against a government is not something undertaken lightly and in a dictatorship the risk of failure is too terrible to contemplate.

At the end of 1938 more measures were introduced that legalized the theft of Jewish property and businesses. They could now be bought at a fraction of their value by the state and their former owners thrown on to the street or into a concentration camp. In 1939 Jews were required to hand over all their assets, including jewellery, before being forcibly evicted from their homes and rehoused in ghettoes.

Jews were to be physically removed from all aspects of German life and all memory of their existence was to be eradicated. The names of Jewish soldiers who had fallen in the First World War were chiselled from monuments and the military records of a further 100,000 Jews who had fought for the Fatherland were destroyed.

HEAR NO EVIL, SEE NO EVIL

Everyone knew what was happening to the Jews, but most people turned a blind eye or chose to believe the rumours that they were going to be deported. Many harboured such delusions until the Allies liberated the death camps in 1945 and the awful truth was revealed for all to see. But other individuals witnessed the persecution of the Jews at first hand in the early years of the regime. They soon began to realize the awful truth regarding the fate of the millions of Jews that had gone missing.

German housewife Christabel Bielenberg, whose husband was later executed for his part in the July plot to assassinate Hitler, is still haunted by the memory of the night she was asked to shelter a Jewish couple. She took them in against the advice of a neighbour, who was also a co-conspirator. Her neighbour reminded her that by taking the Jews in she risked not only her own life and that of her husband but also those of their children, who would undoubtedly be sent to a concentration camp if the Gestapo found out. Nevertheless she made the couple as comfortable as she could in the cellar.

'I simply could not say "no",' she remembers.

The Jews stayed for two days. On the morning of the third day Christabel went down into the cellar to find the couple had gone. But not before they had cleaned and tidied up so that no trace of their stay would give their host away.

Some days later she learned that they had been caught buying a ticket at a railway station and had then been transported to Auschwitz.

'I realized then that Hitler had turned me into a murderer,' she said.

Half a million Jews possessed German citizenship in 1933. Many of them would have been assimilated into German society through intermarriage if the Nazis had not systematically murdered them. Some had the foresight to realize what fate awaited them at the hands of the regime and were fortunate enough to be allowed to emigrate to Britain or America. These included the scientist Albert Einstein and film-makers Alexander Korda, Fritz Lang and Michael Curtisz, as well as the actor Peter Lorre. In total 280,000 Jews managed to flee to safety.

Many ordinary citizens remained, however, either because they did not want to leave their families or because they had been denied visas to emigrate. Many countries limited the number of refugees they would take and not everyone who wanted to flee was allowed to do so. A few even clung to the belief that the Nazis would not harm them but would resettle them in the east. There were even some who were at first blind to Hitler's true intentions.

In his diary for March 1933, the playwright Erich Ebermayer recorded a meeting with the young widow of his former teacher. He expressed surprise at her naivety regarding the Nazis. '… the young widow is not at all opposed to the Nazis. On the contrary, she lectures us on the outstanding qualities of Adolf Hitler, on the greatness of the age which we are allowed to witness, on the national rebirth and is firmly convinced that no harm whatever will come to educated Jews in Germany. I am hardly capable of comprehending this degree of delusion… Nor does this seem to be an isolated case. Not long ago I was witness to a scene in Leipzig, in which the wife of Supreme Court Councillor Simonson, baptized and fully and obviously Jewish, told my father apropos of Hitler's latest Reichstag speech, "Isn't he like a saviour?" My stomach did a turn...'

THE JEWS ARE OUR DESTRUCTION

It was not until 1941 that the regime's Jewish strategy moved from discrimination to extermination. In November of that year the leadership's policy was made explicit in an article penned by Goebbels. He affirmed that he shared his Führer's paranoia and made it clear that anyone who assisted the Jews would be treated as a traitor to the state.

'Let me say once more.

1. The Jews are our destruction. They provoked and brought about this war. What they mean to achieve by it is to destroy the German state and nation. This plan must be frustrated.

2. There is no difference between Jew and Jew.

> '"THE JEWISH PEOPLE WILL BE EXTERMINATED," SAYS EVERY PARTY MEMBER. OF COURSE. IT'S IN OUR PROGRAMME. EXCLUSION OF THE JEWS, EXTERMINATION.'

Every Jew is a sworn enemy of the German people. If he fails to display his hostility against us it is merely out of cowardice and slyness, but not because his heart is free of it.

3. Every soldier's death in this war is the Jews' responsibility. They have it on their conscience; hence they must pay for it.

4. Anyone wearing the Jew's star has been marked as an enemy of the nation. Any person who still maintains social relations with them is one of them and must be considered as a Jew himself and treated as such. He deserves the contempt of the entire nation which he has deserted in its gravest hour to join the side of those who hate it.

5. The Jews enjoy the protection of the enemy nations. No further proof is needed of their destructive role among our people.

6. The Jews are the messengers of the enemy in our midst. Anyone joining them is going over to the enemy in time of war.

7. The Jews have no claim to pretend to have rights equal to ours. Wherever they want to open their mouths in the streets, in the lines in front of the stores, or in public transportation they are to be silenced. They are to be silenced not only because they are wrong on principle, but because they are Jews and have no voice in the community.

8. If Jews pull a sentimental act for you bear in mind that they are speculating on your forgetfulness. Show them immediately that you see right through them and punish them with contempt.

9. A decent enemy after his defeat deserves

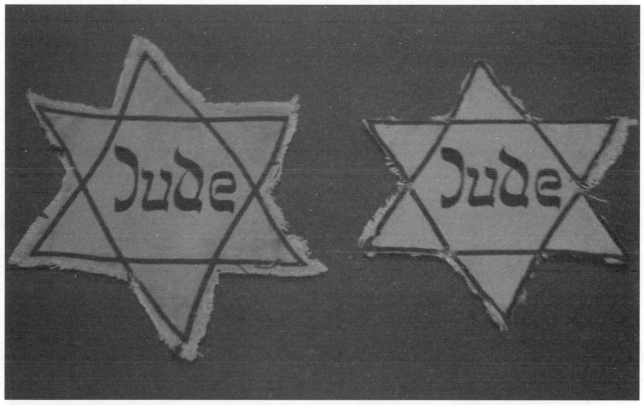

After the invasion of Poland in 1939, Jews were required to wear a Star of David. This was reinforced in September 1941 with a decree signed by Richard Heydrich, Hitler's handsome executioner

our generosity. But the Jew is no decent enemy. He only pretends to be one.

10. The Jews are to blame for this war. The treatment we give them does them no wrong. They have more than deserved it...'[25]

But perhaps the most revealing example of the Nazi mentality at work is to be found in a speech made by Himmler to a group of SS leaders in Posen in 1943. The Reichsführer was attempting to justify the cold-blooded murder of millions.

'Let me, in all frankness, mention a terribly hard chapter to you. Among ourselves we can openly talk about it, though we will never speak a word of it in public... I am speaking about the evacuation of the Jews, the extermination of the Jewish people. That is one of those things where the words come so easily.

'"The Jewish people will be exterminated," says every party member. Of course. It's in our programme. Exclusion of the Jews, extermination. We'll take care of it. ... Most of you will know what it means to see 100 corpses together, or 500, or 1,000. To have made one's way through that and – some instances of human weakness aside – to have remained a decent person throughout, that is what has made us hard. That is a page of glory in our history that never has been and never will be written...

'We had the moral right and the duty toward our nation to kill this people which wished to kill us... we were exterminating a bacillus... we can say that we fulfilled this heaviest of tasks in love to our people. And we suffered no harm in our essence, in our soul, in our character...'[26]

CHAPTER NINE

INDOCTRINATION AND IDEOLOGY

NAZIFICATION

The Nazification of the nation was not achieved by intimidation alone. Conversion was a major factor. Nazi ideology was assimilated with enthusiasm when cultural groups and academic institutions were encouraged to 'align' themselves with the party (a process known as *Gleichshaltung*). Every professional association, amateur club and society was expected to promote the party's *völkisch* values and work together for the greater good. The regime was evil, but it deceived many decent people into working for it by including appealing goals in its programme.

The central aspiration of the programme was the creation of a classless society. Until the Nazis initiated their *Volks* community programme Germany was strictly hierarchical. Only sons and daughters of the titled and the wealthy were permitted to enrol at universities, for example, while the majority of the officers in the armed forces were drawn from aristocratic families. Under the Nazis, employers were encouraged to take their meals with their workers. In organizations such as the Labour Front professional people mixed with the working classes as equals.

A family of Jewish refugees flees Memel (now Kaipeda) after the city was ceded back to the Germans by Lithuania in March 1939. In the background, uniformed Nazis mock and jeer

Their master's voice: a carefully arranged group of Hitler Youth members sit round a radio in an empty room, listening enraptured to a speech by Adolf Hitler…

In this way the nation was distracted from the government's more extreme measures. These included the banning of opposition newspapers; the abolition of the trade unions; the boycotting of Jewish businesses; the removal of Jews from the civil service; and the imprison-ment of political oppo-nents in the new concen-tration camps at Oranienburg near Berlin and Dachau in Bavaria. Conditions in these camps were at first austere rather than brutal.

After the war former Nazis denied any knowledge of what was taking place in the camps or in the euthanasia and sterilization centres. But their letters and diaries tell a different story. As early as 1934, party activist Johann Schnur was having to defend the party against accusations that it had unleashed a campaign of intimidation and repression.

'People reproached me with accusations that the Hitler movement was the destroyer of both Christian churches, that it removes all crippled and useless people, that it would dissolve the unions and thus threaten labour's rights, that social insurance would come to an end and that what the Nazis wanted was another war, and many other such things. When I hear these lies and slanders I tried to enlighten people…'[27]

'THE BASIC PRINCIPLE WITH WHICH WE BROUGHT THE WHOLE GERMAN PEOPLE TO FOLLOW US WAS A VERY SIMPLE ONE. IT WAS "THE COMMON INTEREST BEFORE SELF-INTEREST"'

Joseph Goebbels, 'Der Krieg als Weltanschauungskampf' speech, 1944

PROPAGANDA

The Nazis were the first totalitarian regime to recognize and exploit the power of radio. As soon as they were in office Goebbels ordered the manufacture of millions of cheap wireless sets so that by 1939 70 per cent of German homes had a radio and many more could listen at work or in cafés and bars. As Albert Speer remarked, 'Through technical devices like the radio… 80 million people were deprived of independent thought. It was thereby possible to subject them to the will of one man.'

From 1934 onwards all broadcasts had to be approved by the Propaganda Ministry. Nazi foreign language broadcasts – 'grotesquely unconvincing', according to one writer – were aimed at converting listeners abroad, but it was forbidden for Germans to listen to foreign broadcasts, particularly the BBC.

Newspaper and magazine journalists were also vetted by the state. News items and features had to be approved by the state-controlled press agency, the DNB, and any story that put the regime in a negative light, or did not meet with its approval, was dropped. Criticism of the regime was forbidden. In a speech to journalists on 10 November 1938, Hitler made their obligations clear.

'What is necessary is that the press blindly follow the basic principle: The leadership is always right!'

Goebbels kept tight editorial control of all publications within the Reich and evidently felt it necessary to issue a daily memo to ensure that journalists and editors kept to the party line. His instructions for 22 October 1936 betrayed his characteristic brand of sarcasm.

'It turns out time and again that news and background stories still appear in the German press which drip with an almost suicidal objectivity and which are simply irresponsible. What is not desired is newspapers edited in the old Liberalistic spirit. What is desired is that newspapers be brought in line with the basic tenets of building the National Socialist state.'

Under the Nazis, newspapers became little more than party broadsheets. Editors were told what to print and even where to place the story so that items that showed the regime in a favourable light were given prominence. The views of foreign politicians, or news that reflected unfavourably on the regime, were relegated to the back pages.

General Instruction No 674, dated 1 September 1939, was typical.

'In the next issue there must be a lead article, featured as prominently as possible, in which the decision of the Führer, no matter what it will be, will be discussed as the only correct one for Germany...'

ARYAN ART AND NAZI SCIENCE

Nazification had its ludicrous side too. In their eagerness to purge the world of Jewish culture the Nazis attempted to make a distinction between Aryan and non-Aryan art and science. Aryan art extolled the Nordic virtues of heroism, physical strength, comradeship, community, motherhood, patriotism and sacrifice. Degenerate art, as they called it, was that which distorted the symmetrical perfection of the human physique or explored the seamier aspects of life.

The fact that Hitler's favourite paintings depicted scenes of putrefaction (*The Plague in Florence* by Hans Makart, for example) and morbid erotica (specifically the paintings of Franz von Stuck, which depicted naked women entwined with serpents or pursued by centaurs) was not public knowledge at the time. Neither was the fact that Goering had acquired a vast collection of 'degenerate art' for his private collection. 'Degenerate art' covered anything

Hitler liked to associate himself with the classical ideal, which was the basis of 'Aryan Art'. He dismissed as 'degenerate' almost all modern art, including Cubism, Dadaism and the Expressionists

that could be considered modern such as Cubism, Dadaism and the Expressionists, while contemporary representational art (that is, realistic portraits and landscapes as well as sentimental portraits of rural life) would be sure of obtaining the state's seal of approval.

Jazz music was banned outright because it was considered to be the culture of the negro although groups of rebellious youths known as 'Swing Kids' defied the ban. They gathered in secret and danced to the latest American records by the likes of Count Basie and Duke Ellington.

Film-makers such as the director Fritz Lang also came under scrutiny and discovered that their creative freedom was being stifled under the rigid controls demanded by the regime. Lang was called to the Ministry of Propaganda to meet Goebbels, who made it clear what themes he expected the director to emphasize in his next

film. He could only nod in agreement and thank the Reichsminister for his compliments. By the next morning, however, he had booked a passage to Paris and from there he travelled to America. He never looked back.

Curiously, only about 200 of the 1,300 films approved by Goebbels were blatant propaganda. He knew that the public had no appetite for political films, but were more likely to accept his message if it was delivered in the guise of entertainment. The last thing he wanted was to risk a fall in cinema attendance, because millions went to the movies every week before the war.

EMINENT ÉMIGRÉS

All literature, music, film, theatre and art also came under the control of the Ministry of Propaganda. The organization determined which artists, writers, musicians and film-makers were eligible for membership of the Reich Chamber of Culture. Those deemed unsuitable were unable to obtain work if they could not produce proof of membership. This forced many eminent and talented artists to emigrate to Britain and America.

These intellectuals were not so easily fooled by Hitler's thin veneer of charm, nor were they assuaged by his assurances that he had no territorial ambitions in Europe. When the University of Bonn withdrew an honorary degree from novelist Thomas Mann in 1937, he countered with a written response. Although his letter contained a stinging indictment of the regime, his warning was dismissed as alarmist.

'The sole possible aim and purpose of the National Socialist system can only be this, to prepare the German public for the "coming war" by the ruthless elimination, suppression and extermination of any sort of sentiment opposing such a war, to make the German people into an utterly obedient, uncritical instrument of war, blind and fanatic in its ignorance.'

By 1939 nearly 600 authors had been black-listed and their books were burned by the thousand. Some of these seem innocuous in retrospect. For instance, Karl Wachtelborn's *What Is Life? What Is Nutrition?* was considered 'harmful and undesirable' because it criticized the German diet. Then there was Dr Eugen Steinemann's *Basic Economics*, which accused the regime of promoting state-directed capitalism at the workers' expense.

Novels, too, were banned if they portrayed a negative aspect of German life, such as the criminal underworld described in Erich von Voss' *See Berlin, Then Go On Probation*. Emil Otto's *The Devil's Kitchen* was 'offensive'

Two of a kind: a German stamp carried a very similar image, saying 'Two Peoples One Struggle'

because it had an Italian criminal as a protagonist and was published at a time when Mussolini and Hitler were allies. Goebbel's bureaucrats were also easily offended by the erotic adventures of teenage girls in Margarete von Sass' *Game of Love* and yet they did not raise an eyebrow at the sadistic anti-Semitic pornography which passed for political satire in their own publications.

Aryan science was harder to define, but the regime found an expert willing to do it. The Nobel prize-winning physicist Philipp Lenard (1862–1947), who was then a professor of physics at Heidelberg University, took on the job. In the introduction to his four volume reference work *German Physics*, Lenard's tortuous twisted logic damned the discoveries of Albert Einstein (a Jew), while upholding the laws of Aryan science.

'In reality Science – like everything else created by man – is conditioned by blood and race... People of different racial mixtures have different ways of pursuing science. [Einstein's] "relativity theories" were meant to reshape and dominate the whole science of physics, but when faced with reality, they lost all shred of validity... It is a matter of course that the present work will nowhere need to deal with this mistaken intellectual structure... The fact that they will not be missed will be the best proof of their unimportance.'

Such doublethink did not of course survive the regime or the light of reason. Nazi art is now seen as crude and unimaginative – the very antithesis of creativity – while Nazi science is considered a contradiction in terms. It is significant that when official Nazi reference books were burned to warm the homeless of Hamburg, Berlin and Cologne in the winter of 1945 no one tried to save them from the flames.

GROWING UP UNDER HITLER

History is shaped by kings and conquerors, but it is experienced by ordinary people. Only those who lived in Germany during the Nazi era can know what it meant to exist in those turbulent times.

Horst Krüger was the 14-year-old son of a Berlin civil servant when Hitler became chancellor in 1933. He recalled that memorable night in his bestselling autobiography, *A Crack In The Wall.*

Lambs to the slaughter? Hitler Youth members undergo a medical for service in the Luftwaffe, 1943: by this time, the odds were heavily stacked against them as the Germans had lost control of the skies

'My earliest memory of Hitler is jubilation. I'm sorry about that, because today's historians know better – but I, at first, heard only jubilation… It was a cold night in January and there was a torch-light parade. The radio announcer, whose resonant tones were closer to singing and sobbing than reporting, was experiencing ineffable events… something about Germany's reawakening, and always adding as a refrain that now everything, everything would be different and better.'

Krüger remembered that his mother and father were initially astonished by the euphoria sweeping the country. They then became puzzled and somewhat sceptical. But shortly afterwards the belief in a better future arrived in their quiet suburb as subtly as a new season.

'The time was ripe… a surge of greatness seemed to course through our country…'

The first evidence of this renewal was a cluster of flags flying from the windows of the houses in the quiet Berlin suburb of Eichkamp where Krüger lived and went to school. Many flags were handmade, some so hastily that the swastika had been sewn on back to front. Horst's mother gave him a swastika pennant for his bicycle one day, simply because all the boys in the district were flying them from their bikes. It was not a political gesture, rather one that expressed the sense of community that people then needed so badly. In fact, his mother had bought the pennant from a Jewish vendor who was equally ignorant of its significance.

'Suddenly one was a somebody, part of a better class of people, on a higher level – a German. Consecration permeated the German nation.'

There were parades, processions and new holidays celebrating aspects of German life and culture that had not been acknowledged before.

People seemed full of hope and had a sense of purpose. Members of the Labour Service marched through the streets with spades slung over their shoulders. They were on their way to lay the new autobahns or put up art galleries and opera houses. The old decayed heart of Imperial Germany was being ripped out and a vital new infrastructure was being installed. One that would make the nation's pulse race with renewed vigour and vitality.

The street violence and the persecution of the Jews only raised concerns that the unruly element within the party might cause trouble for the new administration. In the narrow gaslit streets of Eichkamp, and behind the green shutters of their neat suburban homes, the 'good Germans' asked themselves, 'Does the Führer know about this?' But the Röhm purge of 1934 answered that question and many shook their heads as they read their newspapers. It was clear that sexual deviants and bull-necked street brawlers had betrayed the party and had nearly brought down the regime before it had time to prove itself. They agreed that it had been necessary to 'discipline' the unruly element and bring them into line.

As Krüger recalls, his neighbours were left 'disarmed, willing and docile' by the thought of being part of a greater Germany. They were on the bottom rung of society and were only too willing to be swept along with the rising tide of productivity and prosperity. Men stood at street corners and talked of claiming their colonies back, of having faster mail deliveries thanks to the new highways. All agreed that it was about time they had their turn on the stage of world history. Their wives waited in the queues at the post office and told their neighbours that it was their maternal duty to adopt children now so

River of light: Hitler and his intimates watch a torchlight procession from the balcony of the Chancellery building in Berlin. Only Hitler takes the salute

many German mothers were having babies for the Fatherland.

After Hitler annexed Austria they were convinced that the Führer had been sent to them by God and some dutifully cut his sayings out of the newspaper so they could discuss them with their family and friends as they might discuss the Bible. Hitler's territorial acquisitions, won without a fight and against all expectations, had given the people faith in Providence and divine justice. The Führer must be right if he could reunite the German people without embroiling the nation in another war. It was miraculous. He was a miracle worker.

MYTH OF THE PERSECUTED PEOPLE

According to Krüger, many Germans of his generation do not want to admit to their involvement with the Nazis. Straight after the war, they claimed they had been a persecuted people – intimidated by the 'brown terror' of the SA and frightened into compliance by the 'night and fog' decrees. These gave the Gestapo the right to drag suspects off in the middle of the night, never to be seen again. Twenty years later, those who had enthusiastically waved their swastika banners at the processions of Nazi stormtroopers then claimed to have really been resistance fighters. They were secret agents and men who had gone into 'inner emigration'; sly foxes who 'only pretended to go along in order to prevent worse'.

And neo-German historians endorsed this revisionist view to relieve the nation of its burden of collective responsibility.

'They make everything so intelligible… all except one point: why the Germans loved this man, why they honestly rejoiced at his coming, why they died for him by the millions.'

Krüger remembers that his neighbours were 'honest believers, enthusiasts, inebriates', but they were never Nazis. The real Nazis were, at most, five per cent of the population. They were unskilled workers, the unemployed, 'born losers' who would have returned to the obscurity from which they had emerged had not the good and decent Germans in Eichkamp and throughout Germany not put at their disposal 'all the native energy, industriousness, faith and skills they possessed'. These honest citizens were proud of what Hitler had made them without realizing that it was they who had created him. If anyone had tried to assassinate Hitler in 1938 there would have been no need for the Gestapo or storm troopers. The people would have executed the assassin on the spot. That was the prevailing sentiment.

Over a few short years Krüger witnessed the gradual transformation of his friends and neighbours. They changed from law-abiding citizens to enthusiastic supporters of the regime. None of them could even claim that they had been swept up in the euphoria of a mass rally or been carried along in the wake of a torchlight procession. They had simply convinced themselves that life would be better under Hitler and they hoped that the rumours of war were no more than malicious gossip.

As Krüger admitted, 'I am the typical child of those innocuous Germans who were never Nazis, and without whom the Nazis would never have been able to do their work. That's how it is.'

His parents 'lived on illusions', for his mother saw Hitler as the artist who had made good. Being a devout Catholic she could not imagine that a leader who had been born into her faith would not put the interests of his people first. Hitler did not tell lies, he did not want war. But when war came and their son was sent to the Russian front they were changed people as they waved him goodbye at the train station. Suddenly they looked hungry, exhausted and fearful, 'like addicts suffering abrupt withdrawal'. They had been believers, but by October 1944 Krüger's father, who had never joined the party and had never understood his neighbour's enthusiasm for Hitler, was openly blaming the Nazis for betraying them.

'The bastards, the criminals, what have they done to us! After the war, we'll all be carted off to Russia...'

It was not until Krüger became a prisoner of war in Easter 1945 that the relentless resolve that had kept him sane and alive through the bitter winter of five years of war was finally exorcised like a malignant spirit. Krüger and his comrades had been born in Hitler's Germany. They had grown up under the Nazis and been indoctrinated with their lies all their lives, never knowing anything else. Hitler had not only conquered Europe but he had also conquered the spirit of the German people. They existed only to serve him and he had stolen their youth. Although one day Hitler would surely be defeated Krüger felt certain that his generation would not be there to see it. They wouldn't have the strength to survive the coming struggle with the Allies. The war would go on and on – maybe for 30 years or more – and they would all die for Hitler, never having had the chance to know any other kind of life.

Even the German language had been stolen by the Nazis. Nothing in the newspapers could be accepted as the truth. It was only when he read of the news of Hitler's death in a POW paper in May 1945 that Krüger realized he was free.

'I could not believe that there was such a thing... a whole newspaper that wasn't made by the Nazis. A real German newspaper without hatred and oaths of allegiance and the reaffirmation of eventual German victory. It was like a miracle... German sentences against Hitler.'

Only in an American prison camp did he finally feel cured of the vile contagion of Nazism.

'For the first time I felt what the future actually is; hope that tomorrow will be better than today. A future – there never could have been such a thing under Hitler.'

Nothing in the newspapers could be accepted as fact; they existed purely to serve the Nazi Party

CHAPTER TEN

THE ROAD TO WAR

LEBENSRAUM

'The reason that for years I talked about nothing but peace was that I had to. The necessity now was to bring about a gradual psychological change in the German people and slowly to make it clear to them that there are things which, if peaceful means fail, must be achieved by force. To do that it was necessary, not to praise force as such, but to describe certain foreign events to the German people in such a manner that the people's inner voice slowly began to call for force.'

Adolf Hitler's secret address to the German press, 10 November 1938 [28]

Three years after completing *Mein Kampf*, Hitler wrote a second, untitled book which he withheld from publication. He realized that he could not afford to make others aware of his unshakable conviction that a second European war was not only inevitable but necessary. It was the only way to secure *Lebensraum* (living space) for the German people.

'Every healthy, unspoiled nation… sees the acquisition of new territory not as something useful but as something natural… He who would ban this sort of contention from earth from all eternity might possibly do away with the struggle of man against man, but he would also do away with earth's highest force for evolution.'

This was Hitler's thinking in 1928 and it remained the foundation stone of his foreign policy once he was in power. He was apparently willing to negotiate with the Poles and the Romanians, but he knew that even if he could coerce them into relinquishing territory he could not expect the Russians to be so obliging. Eventually there would have to be a war with the Soviet Union. It was Germany's destiny to engage in a life and death struggle with the Russian bear to prove the superiority of the Aryan race. If Germany proved worthy the reward would not only be a vast expanse of rich arable land and an almost limitless supply of slave labour, but also the natural resources of the Crimea and the Ukraine. These regions included the vast oil fields vital for sustaining a modern empire and its war machine. It would be a war that the Germans could not afford to lose. Their belief in their own superiority depended upon it.

But first Germany's borders had to be secured and the territories that had been taken from her under the terms of the Versailles Treaty must be recovered. Czechoslovakia had to be conquered and Poland needed to be persuaded to submit to the New Order or be consumed by it. Then the old enemy, France, would be overrun and an alliance with England and Italy would be arranged so that the invasion of Eastern Europe could be undertaken without the risk of a second front opening in the west. Even with his limited military experience, Hitler knew that fighting a war on two fronts was a gamble no commander could afford to take.

A NEED FOR WAR

According to an aide, Hitler had a 'pathological need for battle' [29]. He had once confided to his commanders that the 'need to strike' had always been a part of his nature and that the war, when it came, would be the same struggle he had once fought out within himself. His inner conflicts evidently drove him to manipulate and dominate others, testing their resolve to resist him in a clash of wills. It is revealing that whenever he succeeded in bullying his opponents into making concessions, he always gave his 'solemn oath' that those demands would be the final ones

Nazi-inspired art: three young men struggle to push iron-ore uphill in a labour camp. Everyone had to toe the line and pull together behind the war effort, or face the consequences

that he would make. In effect he was promising to behave himself from now on.

But when he was opposed by someone who was equally headstrong and determined he would became silent and morose and play the role of the long-suffering martyr – as he had done when beaten into submission by his domineering father. Unable to stand up to the old man when he was alive, he repeatedly acted out his revenge on the politicians and bureaucrats who opposed him in adulthood. He talked of 'disciplining' and 'training' them and of 'driving out their indolence', as if he had taken his father's place.

'ARMIES DO NOT EXIST FOR PEACE. THEY EXIST SOLELY FOR TRIUMPHANT EXERTION IN WAR.'
Adolf Hitler

It is significant that he could tolerate criticism by Chancellor Dollfuss of Austria, who opposed the annexation of his country with Germany, but he flew into one of his infamous rages when Dollfuss dared to contradict him. An argument could be made that Hitler unconsciously transferred his feelings for his parents to the countries that he wished to conquer or embrace (aging Imperial Austria and the violated, dishonoured German Motherland being the two obvious examples).

It is revealing that he repeatedly referred to Germany as the Motherland rather than the Fatherland, while he frequently made

137

Ethiopia in 1945: locals salute a massive likeness of 'the Great White Father', Mussolini, who had expanded Italy's colonial territory within the African continent when he invaded in 1935

disparaging remarks about the land of his birth, Austria, which he described as old, exhausted and decaying.

This transference might account for what appeared to be his reluctance to invade monarchist England. He professed respect and shock when the supposedly demoralized British openly defied him. His only fear was that 'at the last minute some Schweinhund would make a proposal for mediation'.

FAIR-WEATHER FRIEND

There could never be 'peace in our time' so long as Hitler was in power. He put no value on treaties and agreements. As he once told his foreign minister, von Ribbentrop, 'If I am an ally of Russia today, I could attack her tomorrow. I just can't help myself.'

He believed that war was the final aim of politics, that it was the natural way of things and that invasion gave the aggressor the opportunity to 'cleanse' the conquered land of the 'unfit and unworthy'.

But in 1933 Hitler was in no position to prosecute a war in Europe. The German army numbered less than 100,000 men, the figure imposed by the Versailles Treaty. Even Poland had double that number and France too had a far superior force – but neither nation had the stomach for a fight. The French, recalling the sacrifices they had made at Verdun in the 1914–18 war, favoured a defensive strategy. So they dug themselves in behind the Maginot Line and waited for the war clouds to blow over. (The Maginot Line was an 87-mile-long [140-kilometre] network of forts and bunkers running parallel with the German border between Belgium and Switzerland.) However, the Poles were not so blasé. They were rumoured to have approached the French High Command with a plan for a joint invasion of Germany. But the French were not willing to risk Hitler's wrath. Besides they still occupied the Rhineland on Germany's western border, which left the Reich open to attack at any time they pleased.

Hitler knew he would give the French an excuse to march into Germany if he rearmed in open defiance of the treaty. So in October 1933 he demanded that the French and the British reduce their armaments to ensure parity with the Reich, knowing full well that they would refuse. When they did so, he withdrew his delegation from the Geneva disarmament conference and pulled out of the League of Nations. He cited discrimination and the right of the German nation to defend itself against aggression. It was a cynical ploy but one that wrong-footed the Allies and seriously undermined their credibility as peacekeepers.

THE MAD DOG OF EUROPE

Hitler's second stratagem was to divide and conquer. By signing a ten-year, non-aggression pact with Poland in January 1934 he drove a wedge between the Allies and gave the Poles a reason to postpone the modernization of their armed forces. This was to prove a fatal mistake.

The following year brought more good news for the Führer.

The coal-rich Saar region had been taken in

'WAR IS THE SECRET RULER OF OUR CENTURY; PEACE SIGNIFIES NOTHING MORE THAN AN ARMISTICE BETWEEN TWO WARS.'
Deutsche Wehr, *official German army magazine, 1925*

part payment for reparations but under the terms of the Versailles Treaty it was due to be returned to Germany if its inhabitants voted in favour of reunification. They did so and Germany found itself with a rich source of fuel for its rearmament programme, which would now be undertaken in the open. In March of 1935 Hitler announced the formation of the Luftwaffe, the new German airforce, under the command of Field Marshal Goering and the introduction of conscription. Both measures were blatant violations of the treaty, but again none of the Allies did more than voice their disapproval.

Embarrassed by their failure to read Hitler – they had hoped that the return of the Saar might have appeased him – Britain, France and Italy agreed to act together to forestall any future violations. France also signed a pact of mutual assistance with the Soviet Union, which in turn signed a similar pact with the Czechs. They must have imagined that such a display of unity would dissuade Hitler from taking more liberties but it only served to embolden him. He then asked the British if he could build up the German navy to no more than a third of the size of the British fleet. Incredibly, they agreed, in the belief that it was better to know what their potential enemy was up to. Ironically, the British were the first nation to sign a pact with the Nazis. Such a move served to offend the French who felt they were being excluded from the negotiations, but political instability at home rendered them effectively impotent at a time when they could feasibly have curtailed Hitler's grand ambitions.

But not everyone was oblivious to the danger. The British military delegate to the Geneva disarmament conference, Brigadier Arthur Temperley was quoted as saying, 'There is a mad dog abroad once more and we must resolutely combine to ensure its destruction or at least its confinement until the disease has run its course.'

But already the tenuous alliance of anti-German nations was coming apart at the seams. In October 1935 Mussolini invaded Ethiopia. The French condemned the action but did nothing to prevent it while the British voiced their dismay at reports of tribesmen being bombarded with poison gas and driven from their land by tanks.

THE FOUR-YEAR PLAN

The argument that Hitler was forced into an unavoidable and inevitable conflict with the West in 1939, or that he only envisaged a limited conflict over the strategically vital port of Danzig and the Polish corridor, simply doesn't stand up to scrutiny. Three years earlier he had instigated what he called the Four Year Plan, which ensured that by 1940 all the elements would be in place for a full-scale war in Western Europe. The first step was to reduce Germany's dependence on imports of the oil, rubber and iron ore that was needed for the manufacture of tanks, armoured vehicles and aircraft. This was done by producing synthetic fuel and rubber and increasing Germany's stockpile of low-grade iron ore.

While the factories worked to capacity to rearm the Reich, the future pilots of Goering's Luftwaffe trained in secret. They were using gliders under the pretence of being part of the League of Air Sports, because Germany was prohibited from having an airforce under the Versailles Treaty. At the same time the old cavalry regiments were being disbanded and the men were being familiarized with the rapid mobility and firepower of small armoured vehicles, in anticipation of the tanks that would soon be rolling off the production lines. While this was happening their commanders were being trained to take part in a new, fast-moving mechanized form of warfare. Developed by General Guderian, it was known as *Blitzkrieg*. This was a lightning campaign that was conceived to break through the enemy front lines, demolish their defences and sow panic in the rear, making it difficult for them to regroup and retaliate.

But before the might of the German military machine could be unleashed Germany's southeastern flank would have to be secured by the annexation of Austria and the subjugation of Czechoslovakia. The assimilation of Austria would fulfil Hitler's lifelong ambition to reunite his homeland with the Greater Reich and it would also supply his armed forces with tens of thousands of rabidly nationalistic new recruits. The swift subjugation of the Czechs

'WE ARE ALREADY AT WAR, ONLY THE SHOOTING HAS NOT YET STARTED.'
Adolf Hitler, December 1936

Those magnificent men in their flying machines: the future pilots of Goering's Luftwaffe trained secretly with gliders since Germany was banned from having an airforce under the Versailles Treaty

would presumably forestall any armed invasion by Poland or the Soviet Union. When Field Marshal von Blomberg, the minister of war, and Colonel-General von Fritsch, the army commander-in-chief, learned of these plans they protested vehemently and were removed on Hitler's orders.

REOCCUPYING THE RHINELAND

The next logical step in Hitler's campaign was to take back the Rhineland – 9,450 square miles (24,475 square kilometres) of German territory bordering Holland, Belgium and France. The Allies had declared it a demilitarized zone in order to prevent Germany from launching an attack in the west. By signing the Locarno Pact in 1925 the Germans had promised to respect the buffer zone in return for which co-signatories Britain and Italy guaranteed that France would not invade Germany.

But Hitler knew that if he could recover the Rhineland, which included the strategically important city of Cologne, he would enhance his reputation at home and silence those critics who believed the Nazis were incapable of government. It was a gamble, but the odds were in his favour. He knew that Italy would not condemn him because it was engaged in its own military adventures in Africa. Also France was going through yet another political crisis (it had experienced 24 changes of government during the decade) and Britain would surely not act unilaterally. So on the morning of 7 March 1936 22,000 German troops marched into the demilitarized zone, to the cheers of the inhabitants who stood on the street corners and threw flowers at the men they considered to be their liberators.

A detachment of 2,000 troops continued across the bridges into Cologne, with secret orders to turn back if the French opposed the crossing. But not a single French soldier could

141

be seen. It was another bloodless coup for the former Bavarian corporal.

His boldness was rewarded later that month. A plebiscite was called to legitimize the move and show the world that the German people endorsed their Führer's leadership. The result was a 99 per cent vote in favour of his actions. Hitler's popularity with the common people was now at an all-time high. He had acted on his instincts against the advice of his military commanders and had been vindicated. From this point on he would assume command of the German armed forces, giving orders that he expected to be carried out without question.

It was Hitler's audacious reoccupation of the Rhineland that brought Mussolini round. Hitler had long admired the Italian dictator, but the feeling had not been reciprocated. When they first met in Venice in 1934 Mussolini complained that the German leader was like a gramophone with only seven tunes and that when he had finished he would play the same repertoire all over again. But the intervening years had witnessed Hitler's gambles paying off handsomely while Italy had become isolated. The Duce desperately needed an ally and Hitler was only too willing to oblige. He arranged for coal and weapons to be sold to the Italians and

Il Duce and Der Führer ride together through Munich in June 1940. The Spanish Civil War had brought them together and Hitler's audacious reoccupation of the Rhineland cemented their alliance

joined with them in the fight against the Communists in the Spanish Civil War (July 1936 to March 1939), which was effectively a rehearsal for World War Two.

AUSTRIA

In the early 1930s Vienna was a microcosm of the political situation that existed in neighbouring Germany. The Austro-Hungarian Empire had been carved up by the Allies after the Great War and fascists and socialists vied for control of the former capital, a struggle that frequently erupted in violence. While the citizens of Hungary, Yugoslavia and Czechoslovakia appeared willing to accept their new status as independent nations, the majority of Austria's six and a half million inhabitants felt that they had lost their identity and yearned to be united with the Fatherland. Forty thousand of these were fanatical Nazi party members who were active in Vienna. They were opposed by the socialists who were equally committed to the communist cause. Fearing an armed rebellion, the Austrian Chancellor Engelbert Dollfuss banned the Nazi party in March 1933, but he could not control the rival militias who took their struggle into the streets.

In July Hitler seized the opportunity to stage a coup. He authorized a plan calling for 150 SS troops to cross the border dressed in Austrian army and police uniforms, with orders to storm the Vienna parliament building. In the confusion Dollfuss was mortally wounded, but other members of the cabinet managed to mobilize the Austrian army, who promptly arrested the SS men and restored order.

Dollfuss was succeeded by his deputy Kurt von Schuschnigg. Like Dollfuss he also distrusted Hitler but he shrewdly gave the German leader assurances that his country would not join an anti-German alliance. In a gesture of good faith he released 17,000 Nazis from prison, only to see them initiate a reign of intimidation and violence. In the following years their subversive activities not only succeeded in undermining Schuschnigg's authority but also intensified the call for Austria's union with the Reich.

With conditions in his favour Hitler

Madrid, 1939: the Falangists celebrate victory, inspiring other European fascists to take up arms

summoned Schuschnigg to Berchtesgaden on 12 February 1938. Hitler then demanded that Schuschnigg lift the ban on the Austrian Nazi party and appoint leading Viennese Nazis to key ministries. Schuschnigg was also to announce his support for *Anschluss* (union with Germany). If he did not, the German army would take his country by force. Fearing for his life, Schuschnigg agreed, but on his return he told the Austrian parliament that he would never agree to Hitler's demand. He would, however, consent to a plebiscite in order to give the people a chance to choose between independence and *Anschluss*.

But on 11 March 1938, the day before the vote, Schuschnigg learned that Hitler had issued orders to invade the very next day. In desperation he called on the Allies to intervene, but neither France nor Britain would take sides in what they considered to be a domestic dispute. Mussolini preferred to sit on the sidelines and await the outcome.

Schuschnigg's only alternative was to mobilize the Austrian army, but he knew that the Austrians would not fire on their German brothers. In any case, the German army was superior in terms of numbers and weapons. That evening, and with a heavy heart, he made his final radio broadcast as chancellor. After declaring that no German blood was to be spilled if German troops entered Austria, he then resigned, to be succeeded by the pro-Nazi Seyss-Inquart. On the next morning the German Eighth Army streamed across the border and took Hitler's homeland without a shot.

They were welcomed so enthusiastically that Hitler decided to make a personal appearance in Linz later in the day. Driving through the city in an open-topped Mercedes he appeared to the

Heil the conquering hero: Hitler drives through the city of Vienna in his Mercedes-Benz

adoring crowds like a conquering hero. Speaking from the balcony of the city hall he told them, 'I have believed in my task. I have lived for it and I have fought for it. And you are all my witnesses that I have now accomplished it.'

Although no blood had been spilled, old scores were being settled away from the public gaze. An estimated 70,000 socialists and other 'enemies of the Reich' were rounded up in Vienna and many were imprisoned. Even Schuschnigg was to spend seven years behind bars. He was lucky. Others were thrown into Mauthausen Concentration Camp on the Danube.

Anyone who wondered what the new administration would do for Austria only had to look out of their window in the ensuing days. On every street Jews were dragged out of their homes and businesses and forced to scrub the pavements by SA thugs, to the amusement of jeering onlookers.

CZECHMATE

The annexation of Austria aroused the nationalistic yearnings of many of the 3 million German exiles living in the Sudetenland on Czechoslovakia's western border. The Nazi-sponsored Sudeten German Party led by Konrad Henlein exploited their insecurity while Goebbel's propaganda ministry drummed up false stories describing their persecution by the Czechs. It was all part of a carefully planned strategy to provide a pretext for invasion. Hitler had tasted the thrill of conquest and was now greedy for more.

On April 24, goaded by Hitler, Henlein demanded complete autonomy for the Sudeten Germans, knowing full well that the Czech president Edvard Benes would refuse. On May 19 German troops massed along the Czech border but were held in abeyance by 174,000 armed Czech reservists. On learning of the Czech response Hitler called off the attack. However, he must have been encouraged by the complacency of the French foreign minister, George Bonnet, who commended him for his 'dignified and calm restraint', while condemning the Czechs for provoking the crisis.

Czechoslovakia in 1938: indigenous Germans greet members of the Sudeten German Military Service on their way to seek sanctuary in the Fatherland before it is 'safe' for their return

The speed with which the Czechs mobilized their forces forced Hitler to reconsider his original tactics. He now realized that the only way to ensure success was to make a lightning pre-emptive strike that would give them no time to retaliate. He was right in believing that the Czech reservists would be the only force to overcome. Even as the soldiers were marching back to their barracks the Allies were selling out the Czechs in the belief that peace was worth having at any price.

The British sent an elderly diplomat, Lord Runciman, to act as an 'honest broker' but he allowed himself to be persuaded that the Sudeten Germans had a legitimate grievance and came away praising Henlein as an 'absolutely honest fellow'.

Believing themselves betrayed by the Allies, the Czech cabinet agreed to Henlein's demands, which of course he could not accept because he knew that Hitler would settle for nothing less than total capitulation. Henlein's response was to order his thugs to start riots throughout the region in the hope of provoking the police. The Sudetens could then claim that they were being persecuted and would then be justified in calling for German intervention.

While the Czech authorities were battling to suppress the violence, diplomatic envoys and intelligence sources were filing reports in London and Paris. There were massive German troop movements towards the Czech border, travel restrictions for all but military personnel within the Reich had been imposed and civilian labourers had been dispatched to sites of strategic importance. There could be no doubt about it. Germany was preparing for war.

But if Hitler thought he could rely on the unquestioning obedience of his military commanders merely because he had rearmed them, he was to be sorely mistaken. The chief of the army general staff, General Beck, resigned when he realized that Hitler was committed to war. Then on 17 July his counterpart in the navy, Vice-Admiral Guse, voiced his concerns in a memorandum to his commander-in-chief. It was clearly designed to appeal to reason.

'There can be no doubt that in a conflict European in scope Germany would be the loser and that the Führer's whole work so far would be in jeopardy. So far, I have not spoken to any ranking officer in any of the three branches of the armed services who did not share this opinion.' [30]

But Hitler was spoiling for a fight. His nature and his standing with the German people demanded it.

PEACE AT ANY PRICE

Unknown to the Allies Hitler had set a date for the invasion of Czechoslovakia. It was September 30. So when the British prime minister Neville Chamberlain flew to Berchtesgaden on 15 September, in a last-ditch effort to seek a compromise to the Czech crisis, he was working against Hitler's timetable.

By the time he arrived at the Eagle's Nest the 69-year-old politician was exhausted after the seven-hour drive from Munich airport. He was not in the best state to debate the issue with a man of Hitler's volatile temperament. Their initial meeting was brief and uncomfortable for both men, with Hitler treating his guest as brusquely as he might a travelling salesman pushing a product he had no interest in purchasing. Hitler browbeat the British prime minister with a tiresome monologue in which he detailed yet again the many injustices imposed

Into the spider's web: Neville Chamberlain is welcomed to Berchtesgaden by Hitler and his chief interpreter Paul Schmidt. Chamberlain's policy of appeasement cost the Czechs dear

on Germany by the Versailles Treaty. He concluded with his assertion that the Sudeten question was one of race and not of territory and for that reason it was not for negotiation. When he heard this the mild-mannered Chamberlain lost his composure.

'If the Führer is determined to settle this by force, why did he let me come here?' he barked angrily.

This unexpected outburst took Hitler aback. He paused for thought then he evidently considered how reasonable and generous he would appear if he offered to forgive the Czechs their sins against the Sudeten people. He could still step back from the brink at this the eleventh hour. If the Allies could guarantee that the Czechs would hand the Sudetenland over to the Reich he would order his army to stand down

and give his 'sacred oath' that he would respect the sovereignty of the Czech state.

Under the illusion that he had won a concession, Chamberlain returned to cheering crowds in London. But behind the scenes the Czechs were seething. In their eyes they had been betrayed by Chamberlain's 'senile ambition' to 'play the peacemaker'. Instead of coming to their aid, France and Britain now gave the Czechs an ultimatum. Unless they accepted Hitler's terms the Allies would not consider themselves bound by any past agreement to guarantee Czech sovereignty. An embittered Benes convened a cabinet meeting and informed his colleagues that they had 'no choice' but to agree to the cession of the Sudetenland to the Reich. He told them, 'We have been basely betrayed.'

Chamberlain flew into Germany on September 22 believing that he had appeased the dictator and that the signing of the terms of the agreement was a mere formality. Instead Hitler rejected the Anglo-French proposals for an orderly withdrawal of Czech troops and police and instead demanded that they do so immediately. When Chamberlain began to explain the impracticalities of such a move and the benefits of the Allied timetable Hitler flew into one of his infamous rages and the meeting had to be abandoned.

RUMOURS OF WAR

Chamberlain returned to London with his plans for the peaceful resolution of the Sudeten situation in tatters and his confidence seriously shaken. It was clear to the Allies that they could no longer labour under the illusion that Hitler could be reasoned with. He was intent on war and he was well prepared because the Four Year Plan had been fulfilled to his satisfaction. The German army had swelled from seven divisions to 51, among them five heavy armoured divisions and four light ones, while the German navy could boast a formidable fleet consisting of two battleships of 31,200 tons, two heavy cruisers, 17 destroyers and 47 submarines. The Luftwaffe too had grown from nothing to 21 squadrons, all manned by pilots who had gained considerable experience and skill during the Spanish Civil War. The German armaments industry was operating at full capacity and was already exceeding the production peak of the last war. Nazi Germany was a nation armed to the teeth and straining at the leash. It is understandable that Britain and France would do everything they could to avoid a conflict. They knew that there was a good chance that they would be defeated.

The British attitude was summed up by Chamberlain in a broadcast to the nation made on September 28. He tactlessly expressed his indifference to the fate of the Czech people by referring to a 'quarrel in a far-away country between peoples of whom we know nothing'.

Having resigned themselves to being abandoned by their former allies, the Czechs called up an extra million reservists. For their part the British could do little but dig trenches in public parks and prepare the civilian population for an imminent attack from the air. A blackout was introduced which required the windows of all domestic and business premises to be covered after dusk so that no lights could be seen by attacking bombers. Vehicle headlights were also partially covered which led to an increase in fatal traffic accidents and crimes committed under the cloak of darkness.

The great fear was that the Germans would use poison gas as they had done in France during the First World War. It was also expected that they would drop gas bombs on Britain's cities. The newsreels showed plucky Londoners trying on their government issue gas masks and giving the 'V for victory' sign in defiance of the Nazi menace, but off camera the public mood was close to panic.

Images of death raining down from the sky filled ordinary citizens with horror. Experts predicted one million injured in the first two months of the war.

Plans were put in place to send the capital's children to the Home Counties for their own safety. They would stay with strangers who were willing to offer them bed and board, but their parents would have to remain behind. The anguish and suffering had begun even before the first shot had been fired.

As the news of German mobilization reached the French High Command behind the high walls of their châteaux, the men of the Maginot Line were put on alert and more reservists were sent to reinforce their defences in anticipation of the imminent attack.

SELLING OUT THE CZECHS

Perhaps it was this demonstration of the belated Allied resolve that prompted Hitler to postpone his planned invasion. A more likely explanation was Mussolini's offer to mediate, which persuaded him to reconsider just hours before the attack was scheduled to take place. On the following day, September 30, Hitler met with the British and French premiers in Munich, under the watchful eye of the Italian dictator and the world's press. Relishing his role as international statesman, Mussolini informed Chamberlain and Daladier of Germany's demands, which he presented as his own proposals for peace. The Czechs must withdraw from the Sudetenland by October 1, which meant giving up its main fortifications and heavy industry, in return for which the Allies would guarantee the new frontier. Although the Czechs would have no say in the matter the Allies assuaged their guilt by telling themselves that they had no choice but to sign the Munich Agreement.

When the Czech premier Jan Syrovy learned of the terms, he said it was a choice between 'being murdered or committing suicide'.

In a radio broadcast to the nation that same evening he told his people, 'We had the choice between a desperate and hopeless defence and acceptance of conditions unparalleled in history for ruthlessness.'

The commanders of the Czech armed forces were not as spineless as the Allied leaders had proved to be. They offered to fight despite the overwhelming odds against them, hoping that if they could hold out for several weeks the Allies might finally be shamed into action. But President Benes had lost all faith in Britain and France. On 1 October, the first German divisions marched unopposed into the Sudetenland.

The Munich Agreement did not avert war, it only postponed it. It was a shameful act of cowardice on behalf of the Allies, who were to pay the price for their appeasement policy in the coming conflict. Whether France and Britain could have altered the course of history by coming to the aid of the Czechs is a moot point, but what is certain is that appeasement did not deter a dictator.

German troops enter the Sudetenland, which was mostly populated by ethnic Germans

PEACE IN OUR TIME

As a postscript to the Munich Agreement Chamberlain pressed Hitler into signing a hastily-drawn statement affirming Anglo-German co-operation in the event of a future dispute. The Nazi leader apparently gave little consideration to the document but Chamberlain believed that he had secured the future of Europe. On his return to London he waved the scrap of paper which bore his signature and that of the Führer in triumph, while the crowds cheered themselves hoarse. He announced that he had secured 'peace with honour' and 'peace in our time'.

But Conservative MP Winston Churchill, who had been warning of the dangers of German rearmament for years to no avail, declared that it was only 'the beginning of the reckoning'. He was not alone. The French premier Daladier was also acutely aware of the awful error he had committed in giving in to Hitler. As his plane approached the runway at Paris he saw the waiting crowds of well-wishers and assumed they had come to harm him. When he saw that they were waving and smiling he turned to his assistant.

'Idiots! They do not know what they are applauding,' he murmured.

16 March 1939: State President Emil Hácha sits uncomfortably opposite Hitler in a reception room of the old Kaiser Castle in Prague. There was no question just who was dictating the terms

Through bitter tears, a woman salutes Hitler after the annexation of the Sudetenland

Hitler's territorial ambitions were not, of course, satisfied with the acquisition of the Sudetenland. The Sudeten Germans meant nothing to Hitler. They were merely a symbol of his authority, a trophy with which to taunt his enemies. He would settle for nothing less than the surrender of the Czech nation and the humiliation of their new Premier Emil Hácha (Benes had resigned in October 1938, the month after Munich). In the early hours of 14 March 1939 Hitler received Hácha at the Chancellery in Berlin, in the presence of Goering and Ribbentrop, and presented him with an ultimatum. He could either invite the German army to quell the alleged disturbances in his country, thereby making the Czech state a German protectorate, or he could watch Prague being bombed into rubble by Stukas.

Faced with such a threat, and the intimidating physical presence of Hermann Goering, the 66-year-old Hácha had what appears to have been a mild heart attack before losing consciousness. The Führer's quack physician Dr Morell was

called. He managed to revive Hácha briefly before he passed out for a second time. A stimulant was again administered and Hácha was reminded of how many innocent Czech lives lay in the balance if he did not sign the two declarations that had been prepared for him by the Nazis. The first declaration requested Germany's 'protection' and the second ordered the Czech army to lay down its arms. He held out until 4 am, at which point his resistance and his health gave way – he signed both documents. Six hours later a column of several hundred German armoured vehicles rattled through the cobblestone streets and squares of Prague. The snow lent a Christmas card look to the picturesque city, but it wasn't the weather that kept the crowds away.

TOO LITTLE, TOO LATE: THE FATE OF POLAND

'Now we are told that this seizure of territory has been necessitated by disturbances in Czechoslovakia... If there were disorders, were they not fomented from without?... Is this the end of an old adventure, or is it the beginning of a new? Is this the last attack upon a small state or is it to be followed by others? Is this, in effect, a step in the direction of an attempt to dominate the world by force?'
Neville Chamberlain, 17 March 1939

It is customary for historians to portray Poland as the innocent victim of Nazi aggression. History relates that the world went to war to defend this beleaguered country, but not soon enough to save it. The truth, however, is not as simple as that. Since 1935 Poland had been ruled by a military junta. Three years later they threatened Lithuania with invasion if they did not restore the road, rail

November 1939: the serried ranks of Hitler's elite guard march with irresistible force through Prague as the occupying Germans enforce martial law following the execution of three Czech rebels

and other communication links that had been cut following a dispute that dated back 20 years. That is, the Polish occupation of Vilna, a Lithuanian city largely inhabited by Poles. Fearing that Germany might attack them if they mobilized in their own defence, the Lithuanians acceded to the junta's demands in the belief that Polish occupation was the lesser of the two evils.

During the Czech crisis the Polish pro-Nazi junta had been offered a share of the spoils provided they aligned themselves with Germany in the event of war. They declined as diplomatically as they could under the circumstances, which only infuriated Hitler and intensified his distrust of the junta. When that crisis passed the Nazis pressed them to join the Anti-Comintern Pact against Russia. But again the Poles prevaricated, in the hope that the Nazi eagle and the Soviet bear would eventually turn on each other, leaving them to watch in safety from the sidelines.

In January 1939 Hitler's patience with the Poles was wearing thin. He received the Polish foreign minister, Colonel Josef Beck, at Berchtesgaden and repeated demands made some months earlier to which he had not yet received a satisfactory reply. These demands were the return of the Baltic port of Danzig and the right to build road and rail links through a strip of land running from the Vistula river to the Baltic Sea. Known as the Polish Corridor, it divided Germany from East Prussia. Although Colonel Beck was a Nazi sympathiser he realized that making those concessions would signal the end of Polish independence. So he refused.

But just when it looked as if Poland would go the way of Czechoslovakia, the British belatedly declared their willingness to go to war to defend Polish sovereignty. It was an extraordinary turn of events. Britain and France had failed to come to the aid of democratic Czechoslovakia but they were now declaring themselves ready to go to war to support a pro-Nazi junta. Even Hitler, the master of diplomatic duplicity, had not foreseen this. According to Admiral Canaris, Hitler reacted to the news by pounding his desk with his fists and promising to cook the British 'a stew they will choke on'.

Nevertheless, Hitler would not be denied his war for a second time. On 15 March German troops marched into Bohemia, Moravia and Slovakia, which meant that Poland was now fenced in by German troops on three sides, with the Russians to the east. It was an indefensible situation. Confident of a quick victory, Hitler issued a top secret directive to his armed forces on 3 April. Codenamed Case White it detailed plans for the invasion of Poland, to be executed no later than 1 September. It was an imaginative and audacious plan – a decisive lightning strike that would be spearheaded by massed divisions of tanks, which would be supported by air strikes, with infantry bringing up the rear to mop up pockets of resistance. The attack to be directed and co-ordinated by a network of modern communications.

But it was not Hitler's idea. It was the work of Colonel Günther Blumentritt and Generals Rundstedt and Manstein. Hitler familiarized himself with the details of the attack and made suggestions, but the only constructive part he played, according to General Warlimont, was planning the assault on a bridge at Dirschau.

On May 23 Hitler convened a meeting of the German General Staff and laid out his strategy. No minutes were permitted to be made, but Lieutenant-Colonel Rudolf Schmundt made a few handwritten notes that recorded Hitler's

Colonel Josef Beck, Foreign Minister of Poland, who stood up to Hitler in 1939

determination 'to attack Poland at the first opportunity'. He added, 'We cannot expect a repetition of the Czech affair. There will be war. Our task is to isolate Poland. Success in isolating her will be decisive… The Führer doubts the possibility of a peaceful settlement with England… England is our enemy and the conflict with England is a matter of life and death… The aim must be to deal the enemy a smashing or a finally decisive blow right at the start… Preparations must be made for a long war as well as for a surprise attack and every possible intervention by England on the continent must be smashed… If we succeed in occupying and securing Holland and Belgium, as well as defeating France, the basis for a successful war against England has been created… There are no further successes to be achieved without bloodshed.'

Colonel Beck was equally belligerent. On March 28 he summoned the German ambassador and told him that any attempt by the Nazi Senate in Danzig to alter the status of the free city would be regarded as an act of war. The indignant German protested that Beck evidently wished to negotiate at the point of a bayonet.

'This is your own method', Beck coolly replied.

By early May, with war looking more likely than ever, Beck told the Polish parliament, 'We in Poland do not recognize the concept of peace at any price. There is only one thing in the life of men, nations and states that is without price and this is honour.'

This was not mere bravado. The Poles could call up more than 2 million men and they had been given assurances by the French that they would attack Germany by air and launch a full-scale invasion within 15 days of the first shot being fired. However, unknown to the Poles, the French had no intention of honouring their guarantees. Their public support for the Poles was merely intended to persuade the Russians to side with the Allies. The French intelligence service had overestimated Germany's West Wall and had advised the High Command that they were incapable of breaching the German defences.

The British were less forthcoming, offering vague promises of reinforcements and bombing offensives against the invader. Their reluctance was understandable for at that time they only had one armoured brigade and five infantry divisions, a vastly inadequate number of fighter planes and no anti-aircraft guns or radar installations to mount an effective defence. The British armaments industry was still in mothballs following the First World War and would need at least a year to tool up and produce sufficient munitions to supply its armed forces adequately.

EVE OF WAR

Hitler sincerely believed that the next war would be a limited one and that it would be over swiftly. His commanders were in agreement, with the exception of General Thomas who argued that Poland would be the spark that would ignite a world war. Keitel spoke for all of them when he rebuffed such doubts by saying that Britain was too decadent, France was too degenerate and America was too uninterested. None would sacrifice their sons for Poland. But both he and Hitler had overlooked the possibility that being a democracy Britain could find a new and more capable leader to defy the Nazi tyrant and that America could be roused to action if attacked. On the eve of war Hitler had doubts that the Allies would be able to back up their threat with action. In the event of hostilities Britain would have to send troops from Egypt under the watchful eye of the German navy and the U-Boot wolf packs that were prowling the Black Sea.

A memorandum written by Admiral Bohm on the eve of the planned invasion of Poland noted, 'In the Führer's view the probability of the Western powers intervening in the conflict is not great… France cannot afford a long and bloody war. Its manpower is too small, its supplies are insufficient. France has been pushed into this whole situation against its will; for France the term war of nerves applies…'

Hitler correctly assumed that France had been exhausted by the Great War and would capitulate rather than become immersed in a second protracted conflict. But if any single event can be said to have convinced Hitler that the time had finally come to settle the Polish question it was the signing of the non-aggression pact between Nazi Germany and Soviet Russia on 21 August 1939. The news of the accord came as a total surprise to the Allies and sent shock waves around the world. It seemed inconceivable that the communist state could come to an agreement with the fascist dictatorship and yet it should have been foreseen.

Britain had been making advances to Russia for more than a year, but had bungled it badly by sending a minor Foreign Office official to negotiate with Molotov, the Russian minister for foreign affairs. He had interpreted this visit as a slight and an indication that the British had no serious expectations of success. Either that, or they thought an agreement would be a mere formality. Furthermore, the civil servant was dispatched by boat, so he arrived a week later than he could have done if he had flown to Moscow, by which time the Nazis had persuaded the Soviets to seal their deal. But quite apart from this diplomatic gaffe, the Soviets both distrusted and despised the Western democracies, who were in no position to offer any significant concessions or inducements. On the other hand, the Nazis were prepared to sign a secret protocol promising not only half of Poland, but also all of Latvia and Estonia if the Russians collaborated.

The Russians had another reason for siding with Hitler. They were simply not ready for war. Stalin's purges of the officer corps had decimated the Red Army leadership and left the rank and file demoralized and lacking discipline. They could not be relied upon to fight if there were no experienced officers to command them. In siding with Germany, Stalin secured his own position and furthered his own interests, but in doing so he gave Hitler a free hand to do as he pleased in Western Europe. All Hitler needed now was a pretext to invade.

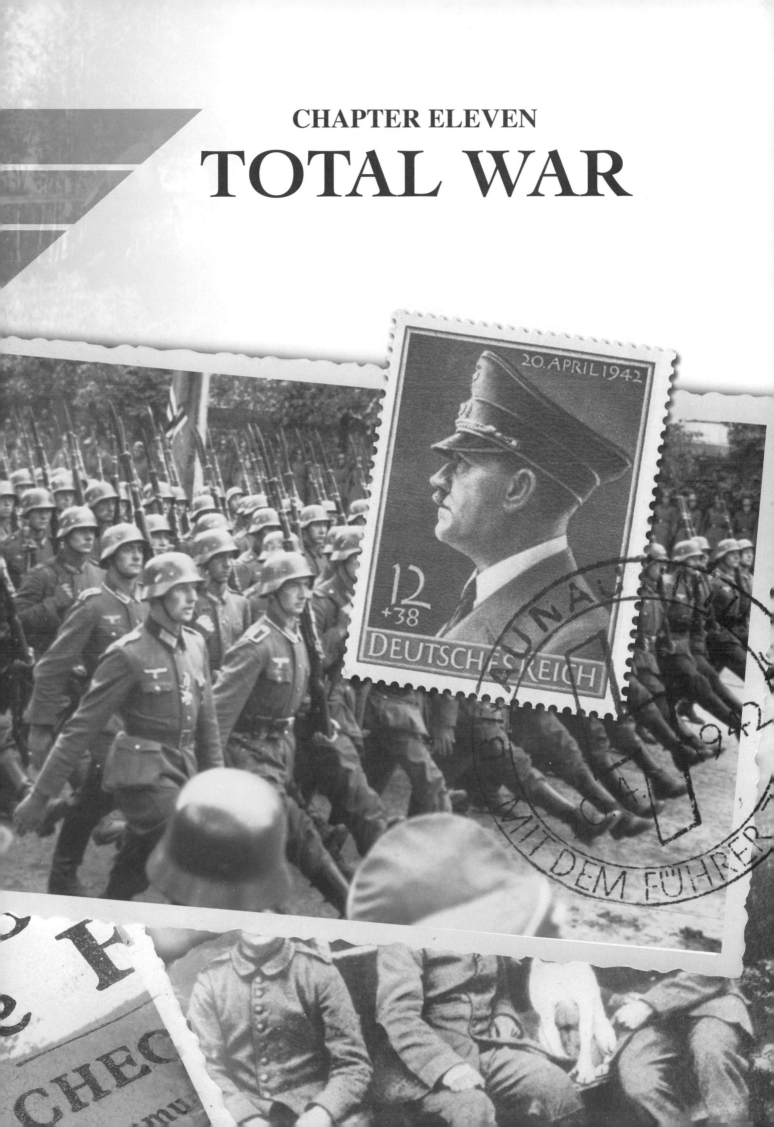

CHAPTER ELEVEN
TOTAL WAR

DEAD MAN'S RAID

The first shots of World War Two were fired by men who were already dead. On 31 August, a squad of SS men picked out a dozen male inmates from a concentration camp close to the Polish border and ordered them at gunpoint to dress in Polish army uniforms. They then shot all but one of them in cold blood. They and the lone survivor were driven to the German radio station at Gliewitz on the Polish border, where the SS staged a fake attack.

They burst into the studio, broadcast a brief message announcing the Polish invasion of Germany and then shot the remaining prisoner to make it look as if he and his dead comrades had been killed during an attack on the radio station. The raid was code-named Operation

Himmler. Now the Nazis were free to retaliate.

Contrary to popular belief, the German invasion of Poland did not begin with columns of Panzer tanks driving deep into Polish territory, but in a more conventional manner. At dawn on 1 September 1939 the German battleship SMS *Schleswig-Holstein* opened fire against a fortress four miles (6.5 kilometres) north of Danzig. The battleship sneaked into port several days earlier under the pretence of a ceremonial visit and was in place to pound the fort the moment Hitler gave the order to commence hostilities. It was 4.45 am and the Second World War had begun.

The famed German *Blitzkrieg*, when it finally came, had a less than auspicious start. While

Swabbing the decks: a German training ship off Falmouth a year before World War II began and mutual co-operation still appeared to be possible.

screaming Stuka bombers strafed the enemy's airfields, railways and military installations, the spearhead of Hitler's mechanized columns became shrouded in fog and in the confusion was shelled by its own artillery. Only one in six divisions boasted tank support – the remainder were infantry divisions, supplied in the main by horse-drawn wagons. But the massed mechanized columns made incredible progress despite the poor condition of the Polish roads, in some cases advancing as much as 40 miles (64 kilometres) in a day. It was a textbook double pincer operation which was intended to encircle the main Polish forces and cut off their retreat to the Vistula river. But their progress had its own problems. On the second day the XIX Panzer Corps led by Lieutenant-General Guderian came to a grinding halt, having run out of fuel and ammunition. But before the Polish divisions could mount an attack, German supply columns broke through the Polish lines and had the Panzers moving again. Elsewhere, the German Fourth Army encircled two divisions of Polish troops in the Danzig Corridor and destroyed them in a matter of hours. It was during this battle that the Polish cavalry made their suicidal charge against the German armour.

Britain and France issued an ultimatum on the second day. They threatened to go to war if Hitler did not give an assurance that he would withdraw his troops by Sunday 3 September. No such assurance was forthcoming and from that day onwards Britain and France were officially at war with Germany. This time there was no patriotic rush to enlist as there had been in 1914.

POLAND

Seven days after the invasion had begun, the German Fourteenth Army was encroaching on

An armoured column of the Third Reich streams into Poland, igniting the war in Europe

Krakow. Guderian reported to Hitler that he had suffered fewer than 1,000 casualties and that it was all due to the mobility and superior firepower of the Panzers. In the following weeks, obsolete Polish tanks and artillery proved to be no match for the fast-moving and heavily armed German Panzers which attacked *en masse*, while the Poles deployed their inferior tanks defensively in support of their infantry. The Polish air force ultimately fared no better. It was thought to be no match for the Luftwaffe. The majority of its 900 elderly aircraft were considered to be useful only for training, but the Polish pilots made up for the inadequacy of their machines with their skill and courage, downing or severely damaging 400 of Goering's fighters. Tragically, the effectiveness of Poland's fighting men was fatally undermined by their leaders, who could not co-ordinate an effective defence because they foolishly relied on civil communications which were easily disrupted by the Germans.

Within weeks the Germans were advancing on Warsaw, but they did not take the capital as easily as expected. On September 10 the bulk of the Polish army was reinforced by the survivors from the battle in the Danzig Corridor and together they attacked the flank of the German

Victory parade: the Germans goose-stepped their way into Poland in 1939. The invasion began on 1 September and ended on 6 October as the country was partitioned between Germany and the USSR

Eighth Army 70 miles (112.5 kilometres) west of the city. For two days they harassed the Germans until Rundstedt was forced to divert two divisions in order to counterattack. By 17 September Warsaw was encircled and the Polish army had all but disintegrated. In all, 52,000 men had been captured and an estimated 750,000 had been killed. There were still pockets of resistance that would cost the Germans dearly, but it was only a matter of time before the last defenders threw down their arms and surrendered.

If the remnants of the Polish army hoped to hold out until the Allies came to their aid they were sorely disappointed. The British were afraid to bomb German cities in case they killed civilians. So they contented themselves with dropping leaflets over the Rhineland, while the French sent nine divisions seven miles (11 kilometres) into German territory. This was a token diversionary manoeuvre and a message of sympathy to the embattled Poles. Incredibly, the British Air Ministry decided against bombing German munitions factories or the newly acquired Skoda works in Czechoslovakia, which had been converted to aeroplane production.

They considered them to be private property and feared the Germans might retaliate.

If the Poles had any heart left for the fight they must have lost it at this moment. However, the fatal blow was not delivered by the Germans but by the Russians. Thirty-five divisions of the Soviet Army were ordered to occupy the eastern border region in anticipation of the partition of Poland. The news of the Soviet incursion prompted the chief of the Polish armed forces, Marshal Rydz-Âmigly, to flee to Romania, closely followed by the other members of the government. After having been betrayed by the Allies, the Polish army and the people had now been abandoned by their own leaders. Nevertheless, they held out in the besieged capital for a further ten days, although they had no food or water and were continually under bombardment by the Luftwaffe and the German artillery. On September 27 the city finally surrendered and 140,000 exhausted and wounded Polish soldiers were taken into captivity.

On the next day the 24,000-strong garrison at Modlin fell into German hands, leaving the remnants of the Polish army surrounded on three sides with their backs to the Romanian border. Within a few days 150,000 men were killed or captured, leaving 100,000 to escape over the border into Romania – but not before they had fought their way through the Ukrainians who had sided with the Russians. The last Poles held out at Kock, a garrison 75 miles (121 kilometres) southeast of Warsaw, until 6 October.

Hitler's conquest of Poland was complete and at the cost of only 8,000 German dead, 5,000 missing in action and just over 27,000 wounded. But Poland's suffering was not over. In fact, it was just about to begin. When the Panzers and the Wehrmacht moved out, the Nazi administrators and the *Einsatzgruppen* (SS death squads) moved in.

'We are not interested in the prosperity of the country... What we are interested in is establishing German authority in this area... We will judge it by how impossible it will become for Poland ever to rise again... What we have here is a gigantic labour camp.'

Hans Frank, Governor-General of Occupied Poland, November 1940[31]

'I DO NOT ASK MY GENERALS TO UNDERSTAND MY ORDERS, BUT ONLY TO CARRY THEM OUT.'
Adolf Hitler, 1939

WAR IN THE WEST

The conquest of Poland sowed the seed of Hitler's defeat. It convinced him that he was a military genius guided by Providence who had no need of his generals' advice. He believed that his lack of formal military training and his experience as a common soldier in the trenches gave him a greater understanding of tactics than his own commanders. He also convinced himself that he had conceived the plan for the invasion. But although he took credit for it at the earliest opportunity he had merely approved the work done by his commanders.

Shortly after the fall of Poland he called a meeting of his senior staff at the new Reich Chancellery in Berlin. His object was to inform them that he demanded their unconditional obedience. During the course of a three-hour speech he told them, 'Neither a military man nor a civilian could replace me. I am convinced of my powers of intellect and decision. No one has ever achieved what I have achieved. I have led the German people to a great height. I have to choose between victory and destruction. I choose victory. I shall stand or fall in this struggle. I shall shrink from nothing and shall destroy everyone who is opposed to me.'

The latter remark was intended to intimidate anyone who might be contemplating deposing him, for Hitler distrusted his senior officers. He still blamed them for Germany's defeat in the previous war and he despised those who had warned him against prosecuting a war they believed Germany could not win.

In the previous year he had sacked Field Marshal von Blomberg, the commander-in-chief of the armed forces and had replaced General von Fritsch, the commander-in-chief of the army, because they had dared to express the opinion that Germany could not win a major war in Western Europe. Then he announced the formation of a new command structure to be known as Oberkommando der Wehrmacht (OKW), which would be manned by his personal military staff and run by General Keitel, whose unquestioning compliance had earned him the nickname the 'Nodding Ass'.

HITLER TAKES COMMAND

The German armed forces were now under Hitler's personal command. Their sole purpose was to serve his will for the greater glory of Germany. Where did he wish them to strike next? The answer came when Hitler convened a conference of the High Command in order to announce an autumn offensive against the neutral Low Countries of Luxembourg, Holland and Belgium. It was the next logical stage, but the generals had expected that Britain and France would have negotiated a peace treaty after having failed to act to save Poland. Even Goering was speechless for once. But Hitler was confident of success. He would rely on the same tactics that had brought victory in Poland – a decisive thrust by massed armoured divisions across the countryside, bypassing the towns so that the Panzers did not become trapped in the narrow streets. General von Brauchitsch reminded the Führer that only five armoured divisions were available, that munitions were seriously depleted after the Polish campaign and that an autumn offensive across open country-side would be certain to become bogged down in mud. Hitler replied curtly that it would rain on the enemy too.

In the event bad weather persuaded him to postpone the attack until spring, but his decision was also influenced by Russia's ill-considered invasion of Finland in November 1939, which foundered when the Finns proved surprisingly resilient. Hitler felt obliged to go to the aid of the Soviets. His thinking was that if he did not act decisively the British might intervene, cutting off Germany's supplies of iron ore from Sweden and threatening the German fleet in the Baltic.

The Finnish ski troops put up formidable opposition, but they were eventually crushed by sheer weight of numbers. At this point the Norwegian government made it known that they would not put up a struggle. They had seen what the Luftwaffe had done to Warsaw and Belgrade and they did not want the same fate to befall Oslo, but they couldn't prevent the British from landing at the port of Narvik and mining Norwegian waters.

The Norwegian campaign suited Neville Chamberlain, who wanted to keep the war at a safe distance. Even at this late hour he still hoped that Hitler might be deposed if the clash of armies could be postponed long enough.

But Hitler was in it to the end. He had insisted on planning the Norwegian campaign personally, stubbornly refusing any advice from Brauchitsch. But this almost resulted in the first German defeat of the war. Although the British plan had been improvised at short notice the Royal Navy managed to sink ten German destroyers and pin the German troops down in the hills above Narvik.

But the British troops had landed without heavy weapons, maps or skis, which were essential in that terrain, even in early spring when the battle was at its height. Unable to pursue the Germans across the snow, the British kept to the main roads and were forced to retreat every time they encountered the enemy, who held positions in the surrounding hills. Meanwhile screaming Stukas dive-bombed the

British destroyers, their presence proving decisive. The lesson of Norway was clear: air supremacy won battles, not seapower. After six weeks of bitter fighting the Royal Navy limped home and Norway fell to the German forces.

The bulk of the British Expeditionary Force was captured and immediately paraded before the Nazi newsreel cameras, while Hitler characteristically took the credit. Victory was achieved against a determined enemy, he told his inner circle, 'because there was a man

Winston Churchill on the steps of 10 Downing Street after hearing about the invasion of Poland

like me who did not know the word impossible'.

General Warlimont's verdict was somewhat different. He observed that the incident exposed Hitler's 'deficiencies of character and military knowledge'. General Jodl had to intercept the Führer's contradictory orders because he was creating 'chaos in the command system'.

Earlier he had reasoned with the Führer, urging him to have faith in his commanders and not to consider a battle as lost until the last shot had been fired.

The Norwegian adventure also reflected badly on Winston Churchill, who was then First Lord of the Admiralty and the man chiefly responsible for planning the campaign. But it was Chamberlain who was finally driven from office on 9 May 1940 by an outraged House of Commons that had lost patience with his appeasement policy. His successor would have to be a man who possessed the courage to take the fight to the enemy in North Africa and the Mediterranean, a man with a gift for oratory that would inspire the nation in its darkest hour. That man was Churchill.

BLITZKRIEG

The spectre of near defeat in Norway haunted Hitler through the winter of 1940 and into the new year, prompting him to revise his original plan for the attack on Western Europe. He thought it likely that the Allies would anticipate his opening gambit because it was the same strategy employed by the German army in 1914. Besides, he had overlooked practical considerations such as the network of canals and rivers in the Low Countries, which could impede the progress of his armour. While he brooded on the problem, news reached him that one of his staff officers had been captured after his plane had

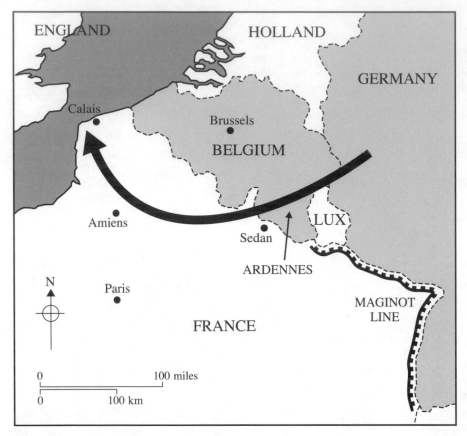

Blitzkrieg in the west: Manstein's plan to attack through the Ardennes had originally been considered too risky, but eventually proved decisive

columns raced toward the Meuse river near Sedan, which was held by a comparatively small French force. Then it was westwards across the plains of northern France to the channel ports of Calais and Le Havre. This would surprise the British Expeditionary Force, which was expecting an attack through Belgium. Speed was of the essence. The armour must strike hard and fast and on no account should the commanders be tempted to disperse their forces or risk losing the initiative.

German Military Intelligence confirmed that the narrow winding roads through the Ardennes were wide enough for the tanks, but there was a chance that the Allies might learn of the plan before the offensive could begin. They could then mount a decent defence. If they did so, the German armour could be brought to a grinding halt and the Panzers picked off one at a time. It was a desperate gamble, but Hitler thrived on taking risks and was willing to try it.

On the afternoon of 9 May 1940 he boarded the Führer Special, an armoured train that had served as his headquarters during the Polish campaign. From Berlin the train travelled to the Belgian border where a car waited to take the dictator a short distance to the Felsennest, a complex of bunkers and spartan living quarters that had been blasted out of a hilltop. It was from here, at 5.35 am the next morning that

crashed in Belgium. He had been carrying with him the plans for the invasion. Assuming that the maps and documents had fallen into enemy hands, Hitler ordered his commanders to come up with a new plan, one that would catch the Allies off guard.

Coincidentally, a talented staff officer, Major-General von Manstein, had drawn up a detailed and audacious plan for an attack on France through the Low Countries, but it had been shelved by his superiors who had considered it impractical. Now they were forced to dust it off and present it to the Führer as a viable alternative. Manstein proposed a decisive thrust by massed armour through the Forest of the Ardennes, which was considered virtually impenetrable and therefore would be lightly defended. This manoeuvre would also avoid the problem of the Maginot Line, which would simply be circumvented as the mechanized

Hitler watched as German bombers, fighters and transport planes blackened the sky as far as the eye could see. At the same time, columns of tanks and armoured vehicles streamed through the forest below towards the unsuspecting defenders.

In terms of men and machinery, the Germans and the Allies were well matched. Hitler could boast almost 3 million men who were marshalled along a 300-mile (483-kilometre) front, while the Allies had a similar total – but they were under separate commands and had no cohesive plan of defence. The Germans had 7,400 artillery pieces while the French had 10,700 and the French could field 900 more tanks than the Germans who had 2,500 Panzers to France's 3,400. However, the Germans aimed to use their tanks en masse as they had done in Poland and they had superiority in the air, outnumbering the Allies two to one. The decisive factor would be surprise.

PLAGUED BY DOUBT

The image of Hitler as a mad military genius is largely the creation of popular historians. It is at stark odds with the facts. According to General Halder, Hitler's chief of staff, the Führer was extremely reluctant to take

any risks during the spring campaign of 1940 and was continually trying to hold back the advance for fear that the extended supply lines would be cut and his armies encircled. Hitler was consumed by doubt after the initial successes, which saw German tanks overrun the Dutch and Belgian defences and advance 100 miles (161 kilometres) on the first day of the offensive. Even the decimation of the French Second and Ninth Armies beyond the Meuse on May 13 (which vindicated the decision to attack through the Ardennes) did not dispel his mood.

'He rages and shouts that we are doing our

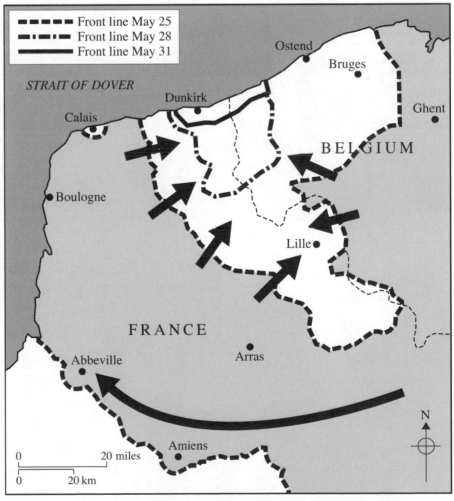

The British found themselves with their backs to the sea as the German mechanized columns advanced towards them

A thin line of troops struggles back aboard a British ship during the evacuation of Dunkirk

best to ruin the entire operation,' wrote Halder.

Then on 17 May Brussels fell. Still Hitler seemed intent on sabotaging his own success. He countermanded his own orders even before they could be carried out, which led many senior officers to ignore them and instead rely on their own judgement. On several occasions Hitler ordered the Panzers to halt when they should have pushed onwards. His most critical error was in allowing the British to evacuate 338,226 men (including 139,000 French troops) from the beaches of Dunkirk while the Panzer commanders watched in frustration from a few miles away. They were forbidden to fire on the stranded soldiers. When questioned, the Führer refused to explain his extraordinary decision, though it was thought that he was afraid that the tanks would become sitting targets in the sand. He trusted Goering to strafe the soldiers on the beach, but the Luftwaffe was too busy fending off the RAF to harass the troops on the ground. It was the gravest tactical error Hitler made prior to the invasion of Russia, for those same troops

would return years later as part of the invasion force that would liberate Italy, North Africa and finally Western Europe.

But even this blunder was forgiven when France fell three weeks later. Its leaders were afforded the final humiliation of having to sign the surrender at Compiègne, in the same railway carriage in which they had received the German delegation in 1918.

'My country has been defeated. This is the result of 30 years of Marxism,' Marshal Pétain exclaimed.

But the rout of the once formidable French army had been inevitable. They were led by tired old men (General Gamelin was 68 years old and General Weygand, his successor, was 72) whose tactics dated back to 1914, not 1940. And all were infected with the fatal affliction of defeatism. It weakened the head and swiftly worked its way through the entire system so that the soldiers threw down their weapons at the first sight of serious fighting and accepted the inevitable – occupation.

In just 46 days the German army had conquered Western Europe and sent the British scurrying across the sea to lick their wounds and mourn the loss of 100,000 Allied troops (with an additional 2 million interred in German POW camps for the duration). The Wehrmacht had lost just 27,000 men, with 18,000 more missing in action. Standing before the Eiffel Tower Hitler felt justified in proclaiming himself 'the greatest strategic genius of all time'. But not all of his associates agreed with him. In private they complained that he lacked the temperament required of a great commander. He was unpredictable, erratic and too distrustful to delegate authority. To the Prussian officer elite he was still a jumped-up Austrian corporal whose

Three days after the armistice Hitler visited Paris in 1940. He thought about blowing up the city, but reconsidered: 'When we are finished with Berlin, Paris will be but a pale shadow, so why destroy it?'

instincts and luck had given Germany a string of unprecedented victories: but how long, they wondered, would his luck hold out?

THE BULLDOG SPIRIT

Hitler had been elated and greatly relieved by the speed of his victories in the western campaign, but no matter how fortunate or favoured by fate the Führer believed himself to be, he could not savour his success following the fall of France. His was the dilemma of the common man who would be king. The fate of millions lay in his hands, a vast army was his to command. He was feted and feared in equal measure, but at the very summit of his success he was alone, at the mercy of his own volatile nature, tormented by the twin demons of self-doubt and indecision.

In June 1940, with Britain defiant but practically defenceless, Hitler sanctioned Operation Sealion, the seaborne invasion of the British Isles. After committing half a million men and several hundred tanks to the operation he then postponed it in the mistaken belief that the Royal Navy and the RAF could repulse his mighty armada. It would be vulnerable to attack as it crossed the notoriously unpredictable English Channel, he thought. The invasion, he decided, was to be launched only as a 'last resort'.

Hitler feared that a single defeat would destroy the image of the Wehrmacht's invincibility. He preferred to play it safe, to have his bombers harass the depleted Royal Navy and pound the Channel ports before turning their attention to obliterating the British airfields. At the same time, his fighters would swat the celebrated Spitfires and Hurricanes from the skies. He told himself that the British had lost the war but simply hadn't accepted the fact. He was bemused by the stubborn defiance of the new British prime minister, Winston Churchill, who swore to fight on the beaches and vowed that the British people would never surrender.

Churchill, said Hitler, was fortified by liquid courage. It was only a matter of time before the British came to their senses and sued for peace. After all they were of the same racial stock as their German 'cousins' according to Nazi genealogists.

EAGLE DAY

Goering launched Adlertag, his aerial offensive, on the afternoon of 13 August 1940. It began with a Stuka attack on the RAF base at Detling in Kent, which destroyed 22 British aircraft on the ground. Hundreds of German bombers then made a massed raid on the British coastal defences and airfields, the first of 1,485 sorties flown that day. Bad weather gave the RAF a brief respite, but the raiders returned two days later. This time radar gave the British prior warning of the attack so they were able to intercept it before the German bombers could do much damage. Goering lost 75 aircraft to Fighter Command's 34 (with another 16 destroyed in their hangars), but as Air Chief Marshal Dowding remarked at the time, Goering could afford to lose that many and still win. The RAF had lost half its strength in France and 100 planes in defending Dunkirk. But thanks to the efforts of Lord Beaverbrook, the British armaments minister, new Spitfires were now rolling off the production line at the rate of 100 a week. The problem was that the RAF did not have the pilots to fly them.

In the ensuing weeks the British pilots were scrambled several times a day and the stress of

Poster from 1940–1, with a marked difference in tone from those produced in Germany

square miles (2,072 square kilometres) of sky. But this time their target was not the enemy airfields, but the docks, the warehouses and the factories of London.

Hitler's biggest blunder, one of the costliest of the war, was to order the Luftwaffe to break off their daily attacks on the RAF airfields while they were still operational and instead target the capital. This gave the British time to regroup and mount co-ordinated attacks on the returning bombers. It was not a tactical miscalculation so much as an error of judgement, whose significance can be gleaned from a comment made by Luftwaffe commander Theo Osterkamp, who complained, 'It was with tears of rage and dismay that, on the very point of victory, I saw the decisive battle against the British fighters stopped in favour of attacking London.'

The change of tactic had been prompted by token British raids on Berlin, which did little damage but so enraged the Führer that he allowed himself to became distracted from a legitimate strategic target.

being continually on standby was beginning to fray their nerves. The sobering fact remained that by the end of August the RAF had lost 231 of its original complement of 1,000 pilots and their replacements were woefully inexperienced. Even when the Poles and other nationalities were drafted in, the RAF was still vastly outnumbered in the air.

'HITLER KNOWS HE WILL HAVE TO BREAK US IN THIS ISLAND OR LOSE THE WAR. IF WE CAN STAND UP TO HIM ALL EUROPE MAY BE FREE… BUT IF WE FAIL THE WORLD WILL SINK INTO THE ABYSS OF A NEW DARK AGE.'

Winston Churchill, May 1940

It marked the turning point in the Battle of Britain for it gave the RAF more time to assemble their much vaunted Big Wing (a co-ordinated attack by several squadrons). At the same time, it presented them with a soft target – slow-moving Junkers and Heinkel bombers, often without fighter support. For the rest of September the two sides waged a war of attrition in the air which the British won by the skin of their teeth. They started to wear down the Germans who

THEIR FINEST HOUR

The most crucial day of the aerial war was 7 September. On that day Goering assembled the largest armada of aircraft ever seen – 1,000 planes stacked 2 miles (3 kilometres) deep, which blackened 800

began to lose morale faster than they lost their comrades.

On October 12, after the Luftwaffe had suffered their severest losses to date and the bombing of London had been answered by repeated raids on Berlin and other German cities, Hitler cancelled Operation Sealion and turned his attention to Russia. Unwilling to admit defeat he told his pilots that the raids on London had been simply 'camouflage' for the forthcoming Russian campaign.

He had seriously underestimated the will of the British to resist tyranny and he had also been foolish in putting his faith in Goering's Luftwaffe. It could boast superiority in numbers, but its fighters were out-manoeuvred by the superior Spitfires, which were able to return to their bases to refuel before rejoining the battle. The German fighters, on the other hand, could only engage in aerial combat for ten minutes before their fuel ran short. If the German flyers were shot down and survived they would be imprisoned for the duration, while the RAF pilots could rejoin their squadron that same day.

The Germans were at another disadvantage. They were unaware that their formations were being monitored by radar, Britain's top secret weapon, which gave the thinly-stretched RAF squadrons ample warning of an attack. They could then intercept the enemy before they struck their targets. It has been said that radar won the Battle of Britain, but victory was still very much dependent on the pilots.

Churchill very neatly summed up the feelings of a grateful nation when he paid tribute to the courageous pilots who had repulsed the invader against overwhelming odds. 'Never in the field of human conflict was so much owed by so many to so few.'

BATTLE FOR THE BALKANS

In October 1940 Mussolini began an ill-advised invasion of Albania as a stepping stone for an assault on Greece. However, the attack on Greece was poorly planned and executed. It left the Italian troops struggling to secure a foothold on the mainland and it prompted the British to occupy the islands of Crete and Lemnos in preparation for a counter-offensive. Their presence threatened the balance of power in the Balkans and put their planes within striking distance of the Romanian oilfields that Hitler had just acquired from his new axis ally, dictator Ion Antonescu.

Reluctantly, Hitler was forced to come to Mussolini's aid. In early 1941 he allocated ten divisions to Greece and dedicated a substantial force of 25,000 paratroopers to the taking of Crete, the largest airborne assault force ever assembled. But while they were being briefed he decided to secure Yugoslavia by force before the pro-British Serbs could wrest control of the country from the pro-German Croats. On March 26, before he could do so, Serbian officers of the Yugoslav armed forces staged a coup. Hitler was incandescent with rage so he ordered the total destruction of Belgrade by means of an offensive that was codenamed Operation Punishment. The new Yugoslavian government was practically defenceless. When it dispatched planes to intercept the first wave of more than 300 German bombers they were shot down by their own anti-aircraft batteries – the Yugoslavs were using Messerschmitt Me 109s bought from the Germans.

In the confusion a tiny force of German soldiers without tank support was able to walk into the smouldering ruins of the capital and take it from the startled, shell-shocked

Montgomery gave the beleagured British the will to defeat the Desert Fox

defenders, who threw down their arms and surrendered. When the final reckoning was made the German High Command was startled to discover that they had captured the entire country with the loss of only 151 men killed and just 400 wounded.

THE DESERT FOX

In February 1941 Hitler dispatched one of his most able and talented tacticians, General Erwin Rommel, to rescue his Italian ally who was struggling in the vast desert of North Africa. Mussolini had invaded Libya not so much for tactical reasons, nor for territory, but simply to gain credibility with Hitler – he felt Hitler was winning too much, too quickly. Il Duce believed that he needed 1,000 Italian dead to be able to sit at the conference table, but he got much more than that when the comparatively small British Eighth Army under General Wavell struck the string of Italian fortifications at Mersa Matruh, 80 miles (129 kilometres) east of Sidi Barrani. In the first three days of fighting 39,000 Italian soldiers surrendered when faced with two British divisions and a few tanks. There were so many prisoners that the captors lost count and

recorded their haul as '5 acres of officers and 200 acres of other ranks'.

More significantly, the British now dominated an area the size of England and France combined, but they were woefully under strength and their tanks were prone to mechanical failure whenever the rough desert sand worked its way into the tracks. Fortunately, the Italian tanks were of even poorer quality, earning them the nickname 'rolling coffins'. Rommel's Afrika Korps had no experience of desert warfare but they had the foresight to ship over tank transporters, which enabled them to recover their tanks when they broke down or were damaged. The British simply abandoned theirs. They also made a critical tactical error by splitting their forces so that several divisions could be diverted to Greece. Britain's forces should have taken Tripoli first, thereby securing North Africa, and then sent any remaining men and matériel to Greece.

In his natural element: Rommel's tactical skills and resourcefulness were admired by Hitler

Within four months of landing Rommel and his Afrika Korps seized the initiative by advancing 1,000 miles (1,609 kilometres) before pushing the British Eighth Army all the way back to Egypt, where they had started from. For this a grateful Führer promoted the Desert Fox to Field Marshal.

Over the next 16 months the Desert War raged back and forth as each side exploited a temporary advantage in men and matériel. At one point, it was Rommel's absence due to illness that swung the war the Allied way, on another occasion the sacking of one British commander demoralized the Eighth Army so badly that the Germans got the upper hand. In the space of a few months Bengazi changed hands no fewer than five times until finally, in July 1942,

General Montgomery took command of the Eighth Army and manoeuvred Rommel into a battle of attrition at El Alamein. It was to be the last significant British victory before the Americans entered the war. Churchill put it into perspective.

'This is not the end. It is not even the beginning of the end, but it is perhaps the end of the beginning.'

CRETE

The Germans did not have it so easily on Crete. Hitler had made it known that the island had to be in German hands by the end of May so that he could concentrate on the invasion of Russia, which was scheduled for June. His commanders complied, but at enormous cost and to little

German paratroopers over Crete in June 1941: they got a hotter reception than they had bargained for with 4,000 men sacrificed and over 300 aircraft downed. It was to prove a hollow victory

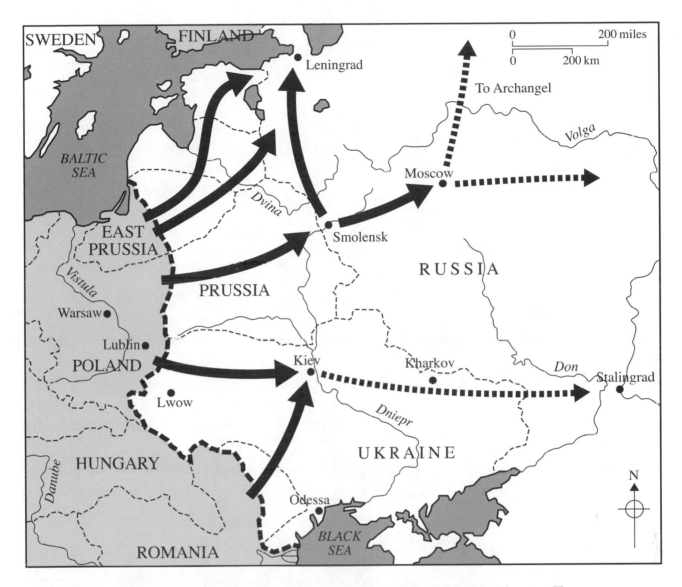

Operation Barbarossa: Hitler's invasion of Russia began well but ended in disaster. He underestimated the vast distances involved and the resources that would be pitted against him

strategic advantage. Hitler did not use the island as a base for dominating the eastern Mediterranean despite the sacrifice of 4,000 men and the loss of more than 300 aircraft, resources that might have been put to more effective use in Russia.

The Allies had also lost 4,000 men, with another 12,000 captured. The remainder had been spirited away under the noses of the Germans in an operation that cost the Royal Navy two destroyers and three cruisers. But for the Germans it was a hollow victory. The German paratroopers had suffered heavy losses and had only won because of their sheer weight of numbers. Their parachute divisions had

proven ineffective against ground troops who were dug in and well prepared. Paratroops only have a tactical advantage when they catch the enemy by surprise.

Hitler declared himself 'most displeased' with the affair, a view echoed by General Ringel, commander of the Fifth Division.

'This sacrifice would not have been too great if the Crete campaign had meant a beginning, not an end,' he asserted.

BARBAROSSA

Hitler's optimism on the eve of Operation Barbarossa, the invasion of Soviet Russia, struck his more pragmatic commanders as naive in the extreme. But his confidence was largely justified. Morale in the victorious Wehrmacht was at its height whereas the opposite was the case in the Red Army, which had lost 30,000 of its most experienced officers in Stalin's political purges of the 1930s. Hitler believed that the common Russian soldier had no stomach for fighting and would turn on his Communist oppressors once he saw the Germans as his liberators. Furthermore, while Russia might appear to be a vast unconquerable continent, it was Hitler's intention to halt the advance 1,200 miles (1,931 kilometres) inside the border on a line from Archangel to Astrakhan. He was going to ignore Soviet Central Asia, which was an inhospitable wasteland with no natural resources. Even so, it was asking the Wehrmacht to achieve something just this side of the impossible. But in Hitler's mind the vast distances that needed to be covered were mere points on a map.

Intelligence reports had led the German High Command to believe that the majority of Russia's 12,000 aircraft and 22,700 tanks were unfit for combat. It was common knowledge that Russian pilots were forced to signal to each other by dipping their wings because few had serviceable radios. More significantly, the German front line divisions totalled 3 million men with another 500,000 in reserve while the Russians were thought to have only a third of that number available to repel them. Something of the scale of the German forces can be gleaned from the fact that it took

17,000 trains to transport the troops to the staging areas in Prussia, Poland and Romania on the eve of the invasion.

But Hitler and OKW had fatally underestimated the enemy's resilience and resources. Stalin could call on 17 million men and several million women of military age, who could be trained to fire a rifle even if they had never drilled in their lives. And there would be no shortage of weapons, tanks and ammunition. Munitions factories were being built deep in the Urals which would deliver the new Soviet T34 tank and the terrifying Katyusha rocket launcher at an incredible rate, while the Germans would find it extremely difficult to replace lost tanks and artillery once they were deep inside enemy territory.

Moreover, the soldiers of the Red Army would not fight for an ideology, nor for their country but for their lives. They feared the commissars even more than they feared the Nazis. There was a slim chance of survival if they were captured by the Germans, but it was a fact that their own officers would not hesitate to shoot them if they dared to retreat. Stalin had even decreed that the families of deserters would be jailed for their treachery.

> 'WE HAVE ONLY TO KICK IN THE DOOR AND THE WHOLE ROTTEN STRUCTURE WILL COME CRASHING DOWN.'
> *Adolf Hitler*

A WAR OF EXTERMINATION

The German plan of attack was disarmingly simple in theory; a three-pronged thrust would see Army Group North capture the Baltic ports of Riga and Tallinn and then advance on Leningrad, while Army Group Centre would

Nicknamed 'Stalin's Organ', the Katyusha multiple rocket launcher could fire up to 48 screaming rockets at a time a distance of four miles. They were crucial in defeating the Germans at Stalingrad

race toward Moscow, leaving Army Group South to capture the Ukraine. There was general agreement that they had to destroy the main Soviet armies before they could retreat into the interior, but Hitler and the High Command disagreed on the strategic importance of Moscow. Hitler saw it as nothing more than a geographical location on the map. After the Russian front lines had been smashed, he intended to strip the spearhead of its armour and then divert it to capture the oilfields of the Ukraine. The commanders argued that the Panzers should stay with the main thrust to ensure the capture of the Russian capital, because it was also the Soviet command and communications centre and would be heavily defended. Hitler overruled them, but this critical disagreement would lead to confusion, which was compounded by the divisive nature of the two competing command groups, OKW (Hitler's personal staff) and OKH (Army High Command). OKW sided with its Führer and OKH advised caution.

If any of the German High Command imagined that the Russian war was going to be a conventional military campaign they were in for a rude awakening. When Hitler addressed them shortly before the invasion he made it clear that this was to be 'a war of extermination'. He reminded them that the Soviet Union had signed neither the Geneva Convention nor the Hague Convention governing the conduct of war and the treatment of prisoners and therefore German soldiers would not be bound by the customary rules of war. The Wehrmacht would not be accountable for crimes against the Russian civilian population. Armed civilians would be summarily executed.

'This struggle is one of ideologies and racial differences and will have to be conducted with unprecedented merciless and unrelenting harshness.'

CHAPTER TWELVE
RETRIBUTION

THE GERMANS ADVANCE

At 3 am on 22 June 1941 several thousand guns lit up the night sky as the Germans poured wave after wave of men and machinery into Soviet Russia. In the central sector infantry divisions crossed the Bug river in the boats and amphibious tanks that had been intended for the invasion of Britain. Overhead hundreds of bombers headed for Soviet airfields and key installations, some of which lay as far as 200 miles (322 kilometres) to the east.

Stalin's pathological mistrust of the Allies had led him to discount repeated warnings from the British and American intelligence services, which had even given him the precise date for the invasion. But he was also aware that the last war had been started by Russian mobilization and so he was reluctant to alert the army until he had confirmation. However, on 22 June he had confirmation he could not deny. On that first day a dozen Red Army divisions were destroyed, thousands of prisoners were rounded up and 1,800 Soviet planes were shot down or put out of action, thereby eradicating the world's largest air force at a stroke. By the end of the first week it was clear that Soviet armour was no match for the Panzers. Although the dreaded KV1 heavy tank had thick armour plating it was cumbersome and its crews were poorly trained. The Soviet tank could take as many as seven hits and

Hitler and Mussolini have a proprietorial air about them as they tour the eastern front in 1942: at this point things were proceeding very smoothly but that was soon about to change

Refugees stream from Stalingrad which is heavily damaged by German shells during the first winter of the siege, 1941-42. Few cities have ever taken such a pounding in the modern era

still keep rolling, but it proved vulnerable to the German infantry, which was able to sneak up on it and blow up its tracks.

Then again, the Russian infantry was a fearsome adversary, but the troops appeared to have no sense of tactics. They would make repeated suicidal charges into the German machine guns as if they were fighting in the trenches of the last war. Half a million Soviet soldiers were killed in the first two weeks alone. It appeared that Hitler's assessment of the enemy might be accurate after all.

As the days passed, rapid progress created its own problems. In several sectors the Panzers forged ahead, leaving their supporting infantry units far behind and their own flanks exposed. Five Panzer divisions under the command of General von Kleist overran the Russians in the south near the so-called Stalin Line, but without infantry support they could not prevent entire divisions of Soviet troops escaping to launch counterattacks on their rear and flanks. The terrain also generated its own difficulties for the invaders. German intelligence had failed to provide up-to-date topographical maps so the advancing armour would frequently come to a halt as its commanders struggled to orientate themselves in a vast featureless landscape that appeared to have no horizon. Adding to the confusion, the maps they had been given were misleading. Time and again the armoured columns would get bogged down in narrow dirt roads because the commanders had mistaken the red lines on the map for main highways.

The situation was not helped by Hitler's continual meddling as he followed the progress of his forces from the safety of the *Wolfsschanze* (Wolf's Lair), his new headquarters in the forests of Rastenburg in East Prussia, where he would remain until November 1944. After the invasion of Russia he made only rare visits to his other HQs – a temporary base in Ukraine,

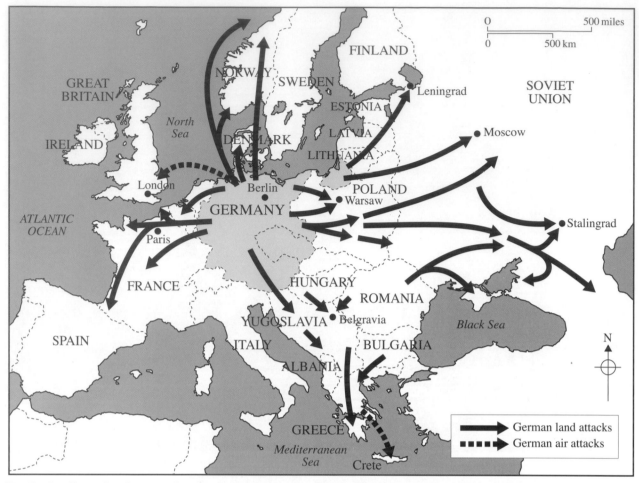

Dark clouds gathering: as the shadow of the swastika spread across Europe, it seemed as if the Nazis and their cohorts were unstoppable, but their forces inevitably became overextended

Berchtesgaden and Berlin. The generals were driven to despair with his continual interference and his obsession with irrelevant details. When they pressed him to clarify his often vague and contradictory orders, he would break into a tirade about the treatment of prisoners or the effects of shelling on front line troops.

Such problems were exacerbated by personal enmity between the generals. On one occasion Guderian, the hero of *Blitzkrieg*, was threatened with court martial by Field Marshal von Kluge, an over-cautious traditionalist, for deliberately disobeying an order to slow his advance when there was an obvious opportunity to push on. It was Guderian again who allowed 100,000 Soviet troops to escape encirclement at Smolensk in late July.

His ambitions led him east to Yelnya (a key objective on the road to Moscow) instead of

north, where he was to link up with General Hoth.

But the relentless advance on all fronts, and the reports of mass capitulation by the Soviets, led the warring factions to overlook such infractions. Any serious criticism of Hitler's leadership was also forestalled. On 27 June Guderian's Panzer Group 2 and General Hoth's Panzer Group 3 put a steel ring around half a million Soviet troops besieged in the city of Minsk, while a smaller pocket was encircled at Bialystock. After days of savage fighting thousands of Russian troops lay dead or dying and 300,000 were taken prisoner. More than 2,000 Soviet tanks were captured or put out of action and 4,000 tanks were lost at Smolensk. Such losses demanded retribution. Stalin summoned the regional commander, General Pavlov, and his senior officers to Moscow on 30 June and had them executed for treason.

But the profligacy in human life continued. The siege of Leningrad, which began in September 1941 and lasted for two long years, cost the Russians more dead than the combined Allied casualties of the entire war. One Wehrmacht colonel compared the situation to an elephant that had kicked over an ant hill. The elephant, he said, might kill millions of ants but there would always be more and in the end the ants would overwhelm him and eat him to the bone.

THE RUSSIANS HAVE LOST THE WAR

When news reached Hitler that his armies had extended 400 miles (644 kilometres) along a 1,000-mile (1,609-kilometre) front in just three weeks he was overjoyed. A week later they controlled an area double the size of Germany.

'The Russians have lost the war,' he told his staff and they were in no position to argue.

Against their advice he now diverted the armour from Army Group Centre, which was then within 200 miles (322 kilometres) of Moscow, to other objectives – many of them were hopelessly unattainable.

'We laughed aloud when we received these orders', remembered Rundstedt, who had been told to take a position 400 miles (644 kilometres) away.

With Kleist's Panzers just 12 miles (19 kilometres) from Kiev, Hitler ordered him to break off the attack and turn south to trap the retreating Red Army.

The capture of 665,000 Soviet troops appeared to justify his decision, but there were millions more to take their place and the chance to take Kiev would not come again. Of more importance, the diversion used the one resource the Germans could not afford to waste – time. When Hitler finally gave his permission for the attack on Moscow it was too late.

When the first snow fell on 10 October the German troops thought it might slow their advance. They had no idea how disastrous it would be for them. Hitler had been so confident of early success that he had refused to provide winter clothing for his men. It was an oversight that would prove his undoing. Then the snow melted and the dirt roads turned into a quagmire. Soon the Russian winter would bite so deep that oil froze in the engines of the armoured vehicles and their weapons malfunctioned because they did not have the right kind of lubricant. More soldiers died of frostbite (113,000) than from wounds.

And while the invaders endured the freezing temperatures, the Russians were secretly smuggling reinforcements and tanks across the frozen lakes in preparation for a spring offen-

Deep within enemy territory Walter von Brauchitsch and his staff pore over a map

sive. They were getting ready to drive the Germans back over the Stalin Line and hopefully as far as the Fatherland. Among the Russian reserves were 40 divisions of the Siberian Front, who were among the best-trained troops in the world. They were also clothed and equipped for a winter campaign. Stalin had kept them back in anticipation of an attack by the Japanese but when Tokyo declared war on the United States in December 1941 they were free for redeployment against the Germans.

Typically, Hitler blamed his generals for the reversal – particularly Brauchitsch, whom he called a 'vain, cowardly wretch'. When the commanders witnessed with their own ears the contempt with which the Führer spoke of his former chief of staff they began to lose faith in his infallibility.

STALINGRAD

With the spring thaw the Germans renewed their offensive. Their principal targets were Stalingrad, a key industrial centre, and the oilfields in the Caucasus. Progress towards both objectives was initially encouraging, but soon the advance on the oilfields was halted by a Soviet counter-offensive while the attack on Stalingrad stalled when the Sixth Army encountered fierce resistance in the north and the south of the city. When Halder, chief of the army High Command dared to suggest a tactical withdrawal he was replaced by Lieutenant-General Zeitzler.

'What we need now is not professional ability but National Socialist ardour,' Hitler told his staff.

Hitler dismissed news that the Soviets had marshalled a million men to break through and reinforce the defenders and described reports of increased Soviet tank production as 'idiotic nonsense'. But it was not just Hitler who was in denial, but the entire Nazi leadership. That winter the German people gathered around their radios to hear a Christmas broadcast from the staunch defenders of Stalingrad, unaware that it was being broadcast from a studio in Berlin. Communication lines to the Sixth Army in the besieged city had been cut weeks before. But even if the officials at the Ministry of Propaganda had told the truth, few would have believed them. They had told lies for so long that no one knew what to believe any more.

Besides, it was inconceivable that the victorious army of 1940 was freezing to death on the banks of the Volga, deprived of warm clothing, low on ammunition and, no doubt for the first time, cursing the regime which had abandoned them to their fate. They would get no help from Hitler, whose behaviour was becoming increasingly erratic. His unusual sleep routine had developed into insomnia and Doctor Morell's diet of amphetamines had taken their toll on his health and his temperament.

When von Paulus requested permission to break out from the besieged city in January 1943, the Führer replied with an ultimatum.

'The Sixth Army will do its historic duty at Stalingrad to the last man,' he declared.

When Paulus realized the hopelessness of his position – he was surrounded by three Soviet army groups – he saw no virtue in sacrificing his men for the Nazi ideal and so he surrendered. Of the 240,000 men killed or captured, only a few thousand saw the Fatherland again.

Hitler's reaction was predictable. He flew into another of his infamous rages and berated the man he had just promoted to Field Marshal as a means of stiffening his resolve.

'I can't understand why a man like

Far from the comforts of home: members of Hitler's 'Invincible Army' huddle together for warmth after being captured by the Red Army in 1942. Many were never to return to Germany

Paulus wouldn't rather die. The heroism of so many tens of thousands of men, officers and generals is cancelled out by a man like this who hasn't the character, when the moment comes, to do what a weakling of a woman would do,' he screamed.

It was evident to all who witnessed this outburst that Hitler was losing control. As news of further defeats on the Russian front and in North Africa (where Rommel had been outfoxed by Montgomery at El Alamein) filtered through to the Wolf's Lair, the Führer became increasingly isolated. He withdrew into his underground bunker, where night and day were indistinguishable, and there he paced his suite of three small rooms with their undecorated concrete walls and plain wooden furniture. Although he pored over maps and reports that made it plain that his empire was shrinking day by day, he could not accept the facts because they conflicted with his fantasy. His initial

anger at von Paulus had been supplanted by a belief that the blame lay with the Romanian and Hungarian conscripts and not the Wehrmacht. His allies had let him down. No one was to be trusted.

His withdrawal beneath the earth was not to protect himself from air raids, which were rare, but from reality. He stubbornly refused to see the devastation inflicted on German cities by Allied bombing raids, which were penetrating further into the Reich and becoming more intensive. In his new capacity as armaments minister, Speer would have to travel to see him. So would the other Nazi leaders. This was something they frequently regretted because he was often brusque and unwilling to hear bad news. Having not seen their Führer for some time it was quite a shock to see how he had aged in the intervening months. He was unsteady on his feet and he had to grip his left arm to stop it trembling. Everything required great effort. When he spoke it was with the effort of a recovering addict. Speer blamed Dr Morell's diet of anti-depressant drugs and other homegrown narcotics for the dramatic change in his leader.

Hitler now ate alone, emerging from the glare of the artificial light only once or twice a day to walk Blondi, his Alsatian, and to confer with Goering, Himmler and Ribbentrop, who had established their own headquarters nearby. Goering, however, was out of favour. Hitler had never forgiven him for losing the Battle of Britain and for his empty boast that no bombs would ever fall on Berlin. Now the Führer openly criticized him for failing to supply the besieged survivors of Stalingrad.

But the Reich would endure. Hitler declared that 1943 would be the year of 'clenched teeth'. He made only two more major public speeches before his death, neither of which expressed compassion for the plight of the German people. The purpose was to assure them that he was still in command and that he expected them to fight on. He left it to Goebbels to raise their morale and deflect blame for the disastrous defeat at Stalingrad. In a rousing speech before the party faithful and invited veterans at Berlin's Sportpalast, he warned the audience that the Allies' demand for unconditional surrender meant victory or destruction for Germany. There would be no honourable surrender. He called for total war. He was greeted with tumultuous applause and hoarse cries of '*Sieg Heil!*' It was the last significant Nazi rally of the war.

'COMRADE, KILL YOUR GERMAN'
Red Army slogan, 1943

REVERSALS

On the Russian front it was no longer a question of how much territory had been taken, but how much could be held and for how long. There were to be no more victories, only stabilizing actions, strategic withdrawals and, very rarely, counterattacks such as Manstein's miraculous retaking of Kharkov in February 1943 – for which Hitler typically took all the credit.

But the celebrations were short-lived. By May Tunis was in Allied hands and shortly afterwards the Axis forces surrendered in North Africa. In July the Allies landed in Sicily, the 'soft underbelly of Europe', and in September they began the march on Rome that was to end with the Italian surrender and the death of Mussolini in 1945.

That summer the tide of the war in Europe turned against the Germans after Hitler defied the advice of his generals and launched a last major offensive in Russia. But even half a million of his most battle-hardened troops and 17 Panzer divisions could not break the Soviet line along the central front. The Russians, who now outnumbered the enemy by as many as seven to one, fought back. They forced the exhausted Germans all the way back to the Polish frontier from which they had launched their ill-fated invasion two years earlier.

By the time the Allies had landed in Normandy on 6 June 1944, D-Day, Hitler was issuing orders for units that no longer existed. Even Rommel and Rundstedt were circumventing his orders, he complained. They were

D-Day, 6 June 1944: American combat troops wade ashore in Normandy in the teeth of heavy machine gun fire. For the first few days, it was by no means certain the invasion would succeed

not only forcing him to authorize retreats but they were also plotting against him. In the bunker at Rastenburg his staff dismissed these rantings as the delusions of a war leader under extreme stress. But for once, Hitler's paranoia was founded in fact.

ASSASSINATION ATTEMPTS

As early as July 1944 it was clear to all but the most ardent Nazis that the war was lost and that Hitler would fight to the bitter end, destroying Germany in the process. Each day the Allies gained a firmer footing on the continent. In the east the Red Army was regaining ground, though at a terrible cost. Their determination to rid their Motherland of the Nazi scourge was intensified with the discovery of each new atrocity committed by the SS against captured soldiers and innocent civilians. It was no

longer a war of conquest but of retribution.

However, certain high-ranking members of Germany's officer corps believed that if Hitler could be replaced there would be a chance for a negotiated peace so that the Soviets could be stopped at the borders of the Reich. Otherwise, the Red Army would not stop until they had taken Berlin. The time had finally come for a coup, for the only certain way to topple a dictatorship is to decapitate it. Hitler would have to be assassinated, but they would have to act swiftly.

There had been earlier attempts on Hitler's life. In September 1938 a conspiracy had been hatched by senior military officers including Admiral Canaris and Lieutenant-General Beck, chief of the army High Command, who were ready to strike in order to prevent an invasion of Czechoslovakia. But Neville Chamberlain gave in to the dictator's demands and the Czech republic was handed over without a shot.

A year later, on 8 November, 1939 a lone assassin had planted a time bomb behind the speaker's podium in the Bürgerbräukeller in Munich, which exploded 13 minutes after Hitler had left the hall. He had cut short his annual address to the Alte Kämpfer (the 'Old Fighters', early Nazi party comrades) of the Beer Hall Putsch because he had been overwhelmed by a feeling that he had to return to Berlin, although he knew nothing of importance awaited him there. Nine people were killed in the blast and 60 were wounded. Hitler attributed his lucky escape to the hand of fate, which had saved him once again.

In 1943, following the German surrender at Stalingrad, dissenters within the officer corps conspired to blow up the Führer's plane while it was in the air. They intended to use plastic explosive captured from the partisans. A package was taken aboard on the understanding that it was a gift for an officer serving at the Führer's headquarters, which had to be discreetly retrieved when the plane landed safely at its destination. Although the detonators had discharged it seems that the cold air at high altitude had prevented the explosive from igniting. Hitler had escaped death yet again. A week later the conspirators had a second chance. Hitler was scheduled to tour an exhibition of captured Soviet weapons in Berlin, which would give the plotters the opportunity to explode a bomb in his vicinity. But again, the Führer changed his plans and walked through the hall without stopping to view the exhibits. The plotters subsequently came under suspicion, so although the Gestapo's investigation failed to find evidence of a plot, all talk of a coup ended for the time being.

Claus von Stauffenberg was executed in Berlin in 1944 after his plot to kill Hitler had failed

OPERATION VALKYRIE

When Lieutenant Claus von Stauffenberg was recruited to their cause in autumn 1943 the conspirators were given new hope. He was an aristocrat and a distinguished army officer who had been severely wounded in North Africa where he had lost an eye, his right hand and two fingers from his left hand. He was entrusted with planning the assassination but his first idea, which involved setting off a bomb during a demonstration of new military equipment, was frustrated. The equipment was destroyed in an Allied air raid.

Another attempt was thwarted before it began. In March 1944 Stauffenberg found a willing assassin, Captain Breitenbuch, who was prepared to shoot Hitler at point-blank range during a staff meeting of Army Group Centre. But on the morning of the briefing Breitenbuch was stopped by an SS guard as he attempted to follow Hitler into the conference room. Breitenbuch was informed that he did not have clearance to attend that particular briefing.

Then in June Stauffenberg was promoted. He became General Fromm's chief of staff, which gave him direct access to the Führer. Acutely aware of the urgency of the situation he obtained two packets of plastic explosive and an acid fuse which he placed inside a standard briefcase. This type of slow-burning fuse made it possible for him to activate the device and still have ten minutes in which to escape before the explosion. On 11 July he had his first opportunity when he was invited to attend a briefing at the Berghof, at which Himmler and Goering were also to be present. It would be the perfect opportunity to take out the leadership in one go. But neither Himmler nor Goering kept their appointments. Frustrated, Stauffenberg gave his report and left.

The next attempt was made on 15 July at the Wolf's Lair, but again Himmler failed to appear and Stauffenberg left the compound with the explosives in his briefcase. All of these delays were putting an insufferable strain on the 35-year-old veteran, who was still recovering from his wounds. But the news of the arrest of one of the key conspirators, Julius Leber, gave the plot new urgency. It was decided that the next time Stauffenberg had access to the Führer he would prime the bomb, even if there were no other members of the Nazi hierarchy present. Hitler was the key. His death would free the conspirators to negotiate an armistice with the British and the Americans before the Russians could enter Germany. Operation Valkyrie, the assassination of the Führer and the takeover of the Nazi administration, was rescheduled for 20 July, the next planned briefing at the Wolf's Lair.

By this stage Field Marshal Rommel had reluctantly given his support to the plot. He had initially urged the conspirators to arrest Hitler and put him on trial so that the German people would learn how he had betrayed their trust. But when his pleas to negotiate with the Allies were dismissed out of hand, Rommel realised that Hitler could not be reasoned with.

At dawn on 20 July Stauffenberg and his aide, Lieutenant von Haeften, boarded a plane at Berlin Tempelhof for the 300-mile (483-kilometre) flight to Rastenburg. Stauffenberg carried his regular briefcase containing his papers, while Haeften held an identical briefcase that was filled with explosives. At the airfield in East Prussia they were met by a driver who knew nothing of their plans and were driven to the heavily guarded compound for the first in a series of meetings that were to culminate with the daily Führer briefing at 12.30.

At 12.20 Stauffenberg excused himself on the pretext of having to change into a fresh shirt. He and Haeften then entered the briefing hut and hurriedly primed the bomb while the other officers waited impatiently outside. It was a hot and humid day, so hot in fact that the steel shutters of the briefing room were up and the windows were wide open. Stauffenberg had to arm the detonators by breaking the acid capsule with pliers that had been specially made for his injured hand. He only had minutes to do it in. But before he could arm the second packet, a staff sergeant entered the room and reminded them that the Führer was waiting. The sergeant did not see what they were doing because they had their backs to him, but this interruption forced them to abandon their plan to prime the second packet. Haeften took it with him and waited in the car while Stauffenberg joined the officers in the briefing room. He was only carrying half of the explosives that he had planned to use.

They found the Führer seated on a stool. He was musing on the maps spread before him on a large wooden table. Hitler looked up for a moment as Stauffenberg entered, then continued with the briefing which was being given by Lieutenant-General Heusinger. Stauffenberg had less than five minutes in which to plant the bomb and get a safe distance from the building, but he kept his composure. He calmly asked an adjutant to allow him to stand next to Heusinger because he was hard of hearing. This placed him within inches of his target. Unnoticed, he slipped the briefcase under the table and leant it against the thick concrete support before finding an excuse to leave. As he did so Colonel Brandt took his place. Seeing the briefcase poking out from under the table he idly pushed it further away with his foot.

A few moments later Stauffenberg was at a safe distance, waiting anxiously by the car with Heusinger. It was 12.45. The next instant a tremendous explosion shook the forest and the briefing hut erupted in smoke and flame. Surely, no one could have survived the blast. Without waiting to see if there were any survivors the bombers leapt into the car and ordered the driver

Shaken and stirred, Hitler plots revenge against those who carried out the assassination attempt. Behind him, to his right, is Martin Bormann; to his left, the bandaged figure of General Alfred Jodl

to head for the airfield. They tossed the second packet of explosive into the trees as they sped along and after a heart-stopping moment at a checkpoint they managed to bluff their way through and board the plane back to Berlin.

But Hitler had survived. The concrete table support had deflected the force of the blast, which was further diffused by the open windows. Had Stauffenberg been able to arm the second packet of explosive the assassination attempt might still have been successful. In the event, Hitler walked unharmed from the wreckage. His face was blackened, his hair was singed and his clothes were in tatters, but he was alive.

It seemed that the Führer did indeed lead a charmed life.

But those around him did not. Colonel Brandt and three other senior officers died of the wounds they received in the blast, while 20 others were injured.

AFTERMATH OF THE JULY PLOT

It has been estimated that as many as 5,000 people lost their lives as a result of the failure of the July Plot. Some of these committed suicide in order to avoid interrogation at the hands of the Gestapo, while others, such as Field Marshal Rommel, wanted to protect their families from reprisals.

The principal conspirators – Claus von Stauffenberg, Ludwig Beck and Carl Goerdeler – were shot by firing squad as soon as their complicity in the plot was discovered. When Himmler heard of their fate he ordered their bodies to be exhumed and burned and their ashes scattered. Their co-conspirators were not so fortunate. Many were tortured to death or hung from meat hooks while being slowly throt-

Erwin Rommel inspects the Atlantic Sea Wall: the Allies invaded earlier than he had expected

tled with piano wire, the spectacle being filmed in colour for Hitler's perverse enjoyment.

They all knew the risk they were taking, but as General von Tresckow wrote before taking his own life on the Russian Front on 21 July 1944, 'The moral worth of a man only begins at the point where he is ready to sacrifice his life for his convictions.'

As an officer of the Wehrmacht he knew that at the end of the war he would be condemned by the world for his part in countless atrocities, but he felt that he had redeemed himself by this belated gesture of defiance.

'Now the whole world will assail and curse us. But I am as solidly convinced as ever I was that what we did was right. I believe that Hitler is the archenemy not only of Germany, but of the whole world.'

Count Helmuth James von Moltke, who had hosted a gathering of anti-Nazis, was arrested in 1944 but he was not tried and executed until a year later. He too, was convinced that he had a duty to try to topple the regime.

He told his sons shortly before his death:

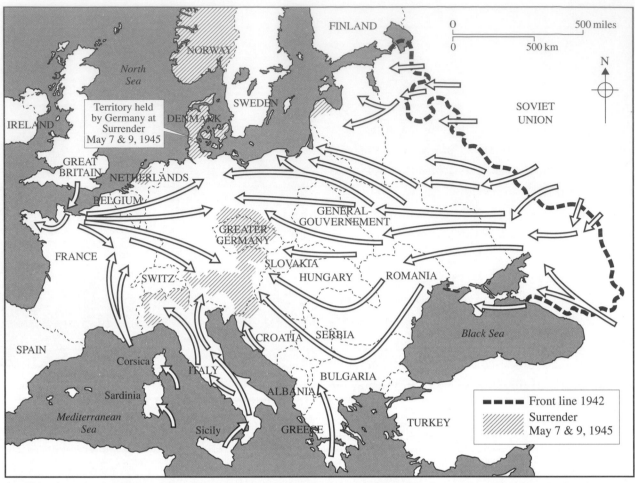

Attacked on four fronts, Hitler's empire was doomed to destruction once the allies fought back. The front line of 1942 had shifted hundreds of miles westwards, to the outskirts of Berlin

'All my life, even in school, I fought against a spirit of narrowness and force, of arrogance, intolerance and pitiless absolute logic which is a part of the German equipment, and which found its embodiment in the National Socialist state.'[32]

Even if the conspirators had been successful in decapitating the leadership, they would have had a struggle to convince a Nazified nation that the removal of Hitler was in their best interests and that it was morally justifiable as a means of averting further suffering. With that end in mind Beck drafted an address that would have been delivered to the press and broadcast over the airwaves once

'DO ENJOY WAR. PEACE WILL BE DREADFUL.'
Popular slogan in Germany, April 1945

news of Hitler's death had been confirmed.

It serves as a damning indictment of the dictator by his own generals and is a stinging rebuff to those historians who maintain that Hitler was a strategic genius.

'Monstrous things have taken place under our eyes in the years past. Against the advice of his experts, Hitler has unscrupulously sacrificed whole armies for his desire for glory, his presumption of power, his blasphemous delusion of being the chosen and inspired instrument of what he calls "Providence".

'Not elected by the German people, but reaching supreme power by the worst of

1945 and a Soviet soldier stands guard over the rooftops of an unnamed German city

intrigues, he has created confusion by his demonical arts and lies, and by his incredible waste, which appeared to bring benefits to all, but which in reality has thrown the German people into tremendous debt. To maintain his power, he has established an unbridled reign of terror, destroying justice, banishing decency, mocking the divine commands of pure humanity and destroying the happiness of millions.

'With deadly certainty, his mad contempt for all mankind ultimately had to result in catastrophe for our people. His self-bestowed generalship had to lead our brave sons, fathers, husbands, brothers into disaster. His bloody terror against defenceless people had to bring disgrace to the German name.'[33]

BATTLE FOR BERLIN

Hitler had escaped unscathed, but the scale of the conspiracy had shaken him. He now regarded even his most loyal generals with suspicion. When he was told that the Red Army was massed along a broad front from Warsaw to the Carpathian mountains, in preparation for the last push that would ultimately take it to Berlin, Hitler shrugged the warning off as 'the greatest bluff since Genghis Khan'. But the presence of 2.2 million Soviet soldiers, 6,400 tanks and 46,000 heavy guns was a cold, sobering fact. The combined forces of Generals Zhukov and Konev heavily outnumbered the remnants of the German armed forces. They had eleven times more infantry, seven times more tanks and twenty times more artillery. This was the endgame. The final reckoning.

Germany was being bombed by the British by night and the Americans by day. Both assailants were unmolested by the Luftwaffe, which had evaporated months before during the ill-fated Ardennes offensive known as the Battle of the Bulge. Hitler had squandered 100,000 men, 800

1945: a little girl huddles for warmth by a fire in the streets of bombed-out Nuremberg

Accompanied by a crowd of officials, Adolf Hitler grimly inspects bomb damage in 1944 in German film that was captured by the US Army Signal Corps on the western front and used as propaganda

tanks, 1,000 aircraft and 50 trainloads of ammunition in that last desperate gesture in December 1944. But it had only served to hasten the end. The entire German reserves had been wasted instead of being used in defence of the Rhine. Even Rundstedt had condemned the offensive as 'a second Stalingrad'.

Now there were not enough men of combat experience to defend Germany's cities, only the old men of the *Volkssturm* (Germany's Home Guard) and the boys of the Hitler Youth.

And these remnants of Germany's manhood fought on mainly through fear rather than fanaticism, for on every street corner the bodies of deserters were hung from lampposts with placards around their necks – a warning to those who refused to do their duty.

Dresden, Cologne, Hamburg and dozens more of Germany's major centres were little more than charred, smouldering ruins, their citizens reduced to scavenging for scraps. Water, electricity and gas supplies had been disrupted months before and the sewage system was no longer functioning. All major roads were pockmarked with craters and strewn with rubble and the rail network was a mangle of twisted rails and abandoned rolling stock. There was nowhere for the terrified civilians to go but down into the cellars of bombed-out buildings and into the underground stations, just as the people of Warsaw, Belgrade and London had done only four years earlier.

The hammer and sickle is hoisted over the Reichstag in Berlin on 30 April 1945. Below is a scene of utter desolation with bullet-ridden buildings, burnt-out trams and shot-up cars littering the streets

And now their Führer shared their fate. In January 1945, as the Allies closed in, he retreated to the bunker beneath the Chancellery in Berlin. Surrounded by his staff as the Russian shells shook the ground above them he was now mentally and physically under siege.

ASSAULT ON THE REICH

On 7 March 1945 the Allies crossed the Rhine at Remagen after German engineers had failed to destroy the main railway bridge. Soldiers of the US 9th Division removed the remaining demolition charges under fire in order to secure the route into Germany. Hitler responded by sacking Rundstedt and ordering the execution of the five officers who had been responsible for the bridge's destruction.

Significant as this breakthrough was, several Allied commanders were of the opinion that the war could have been ended six months earlier if the advance had not been halted prematurely. At that point the Rhine was held by one Danish SS division and another unit consisting of elderly men, both of whom would have been happy to surrender. But the opportunity was squandered by the Allied leadership, who wanted to conserve petrol. By the time the order was given to advance the Rhine region had been reinforced.

But elsewhere the Germans were in retreat. The Reich was shrinking at an astonishing rate. Finland, Estonia, Latvia and Lithuania were soon cleared of the German invaders. In the south, Ukraine was in Russian hands, Romania was out of the war and Bulgaria was free. Elsewhere, Greece had been liberated and Tito's partisans were in control of Yugoslavia.

On the evening of 23 March the Allies launched their last major offensive of the war. The event was watched with grim satisfaction by the British prime minister Winston Churchill and Field Marshal Montgomery. More than 3,000 guns west of the Rhine at Wesel opened up the attack, which had been preceded by weeks of bombing along the Ruhr. Then a million men poured across the Rhine in order to engage General Model's Army Group B. At dawn Churchill insisted on crossing with the troops, who were able to advance six miles (9.5 kilometres) into enemy territory before encountering serious resistance. When victory came on 18 April the Allies netted 317,000 prisoners, more than the Russians had captured at Stalingrad.

Finally, on 25 April, soldiers of the United States First Army and Soviet soldiers of the Fifth Guards Army shook hands at Torgau, 70 miles (112.5 kilometres) southwest of Berlin. On that same day one million Russians paused before they made the final attack on the capital of the Third Reich.

THE BUNKER

'If the war is lost, the people will be lost also. It is not necessary to worry about what the people will need for elemental survival. On the contrary it is better for us to destroy

'IF THE GERMAN PEOPLE LOSE THIS WAR THEN THEY HAVE SHOWN THEMSELVES TO BE UNWORTHY OF ME.'

Adolf Hitler, 18 April 1945

even these things. For this nation has proven itself to be the weaker...'

Adolf Hitler, 18 March 1945

On March 19 Hitler ordered the destruction of Germany's infrastructure, its surviving factories and power plants, its communications network and its transportation and other resources, so that nothing of use would be left for the Allies or the German people. This scorched earth policy, known as the Nero Decree, was Hitler's way of punishing the German people for their failure to fulfil the Aryan ideal.

When news reached him that Goering and Himmler were attempting to negotiate a separate peace in order to save their own skins, Hitler raged that he had been betrayed. At that point he finally conceded that the war was lost. Just after midnight on April 29 he prepared his exit from the world. In a quiet civil ceremony he married his mistress Eva Braun, who had informed him that she intended to die by his side whenever he was ready. While the inmates of the bunker celebrated with cake and champagne, in a surreal atmosphere of desperate gaiety, Hitler ordered his physician to test a cyanide capsule on Blondi his dog. The capsules had been given to him by Himmler, who he suspected might have substituted the poison for a sedative so the Soviets could capture him alive and put him on trial.

When the drug proved itself to be fatal, Hitler presented each of his secretaries with a small box containing a capsule as a parting gift. At this point he was a wizened shell of his former self, his penetrating gaze dulled with drugs, his face sallow and his hand shaking. As he moved he shuffled like an old man. An SS guard observed that he looked closer to 70 than his real age of 56.

GÖTTERDÄMMERUNG

At 2 am on 29 April 1945 Hitler sat in his study and dictated his political testament to his secretary, Gertrud Junge, while the thud of Russian artillery intensified above the besieged bunker. Junge expected that she would finally learn the reason for the war and why it had come to such an inglorious end for her country.

But to her dismay, Hitler repeated the same old arguments that he had used for years. He cynically blamed the Jews for the war that he had begun with the invasion of Poland. A war that was prosecuted with such brutality that the Allies were given no option but to demand the unconditional surrender of Germany.

'It is untrue that I, or anyone else in Germany wanted war in 1939. It was desired and caused by none but those international statesmen who were of Jewish descent or who were working for Jewish interests...

'After a six-year struggle which, in spite of all reverses, will one day be inscribed in the pages of history as the most glorious and courageous kind of evidence of a nation's will to live, I cannot leave this city which is the capital of the Reich. Since our forces are too small to withstand the enemy's attack on this particular spot, since our resistance has been slowly undermined by creatures whose lack of character is matched by their folly, I wish by remaining in this city to join my fate to that which millions of others too have taken upon themselves. Besides, I do not wish to fall into the hands of enemies who, for the amusement of their misguided masses, need another spectacle arranged by the Jews. I therefore reached the decision to stay in Berlin and to choose death voluntarily at the moment that I should feel that the residence of the Führer and chancellor can no longer be defended...

'From the sacrifices of our soldiers, and from my own bond with them unto death, in one way or another the seed will rise in German history and there will be a radiant rebirth of the National Socialist movement…'

He concluded by announcing a new cabinet and his choice of successor, Admiral Dönitz. It was a surreal moment, but one characteristic of Hitler's state of mind.

SUICIDE

Hitler rose at 6 am on the last morning of his life, having slept fitfully. The celebrations were over and the atmosphere in the bunker was subdued. Amid the empty bottles and the dirty dishes the last partygoers slept off their drink. Others discussed the most painless and effective method of committing suicide, with the clinical detachment of people who had known the end would come and were now simply resigned to it.

At noon Hitler convened his last conference while preparations were made for a Wagnerian funeral. But petrol was in short supply and the shelling made an elaborate ceremony impossible.

After a simple lunch of salad and spaghetti Hitler said his final farewells to Junge, Bormann, Goebbels and the last of the inner circle. He was now so frail that his final whispered words were lost in the low thud of the incoming shells.

Then he and his new bride entered their private apartment and closed the door behind them. It was 3.30 pm. But Hitler was denied a dignified exit. Moments later a hysterical Frau Goebbels pushed through the small group waiting outside in the corridor and tearfully begged the Führer to reconsider. She was ushered from the room and the door was closed.

Moments later the suffocating silence was shattered by a pistol shot. One of the Goebbels children heard it from the staircase where he was playing.

'That was a bull's-eye,' he said.

No one cried. Instead, almost as one, they lit their cigarettes, something which Hitler had forbidden in his presence, and drew in a long, satisfying wreath of tobacco smoke. Hitler was dead and his death freed them, as it did everyone else, of his overpowering presence.

When his valet and two SS bodyguards entered the room they found Hitler slumped on the left side of the blue and white velvet sofa with his hands clasped in his lap. Blood was trickling down from a hole in his right temple and his 7.65 mm pistol lay at his side. He appeared to have taken poison and his bride then delivered the coup de grace, just to be sure. Eva Braun lay dead beside him, her legs tucked underneath her. She, too, had taken cyanide.

The bodies were draped in a blanket and carried upstairs, where they were laid in a shell crater by the entrance to the bunker. Then petrol was poured on to the corpses and ignited with a taper from the valet's notebook. There was no funeral oration and no solemn Wagnerian music, only the whining of shells and the dull thud of the explosions, which were now only yards away. But there was one final lie to be told. When Admiral Dönitz announced Hitler's death in a radio broadcast the next day he told the German people that their Führer had died fighting at the head of his troops.

That same day, 1 May 1945, Goebbels and his wife killed themselves after first poisoning their children. They could not imagine living in a world without their Führer. But Bormann's loyalty evaporated with Hitler's death. He chose

Long thought to show Hitler, this photo (taken in the bunker) is actually of a member of his staff

Portrait of Eva Braun, which was found in her personal photo album at the end of WWII

to flee when the survivors broke out of the bunker that night and made their way towards what they hoped were the American lines. He didn't make it. His body was later found on a railway bridge a mile to the north of the Chancellery. He had apparently swallowed cyanide rather than be captured by the Russians.

On May 23 Himmler, disguised as a common soldier, was captured by the British at Bremen. While he was being examined by a doctor he bit into a cyanide capsule that had been hidden in the hollow of one of his teeth. He died within minutes.

Weeks later Goering surrendered. He was eventually put on trial at Nuremberg with other leading Nazis, among whom was Dr Robert Ley, who hung himself before the trial could begin. Goering also took his own life in his cell, but only after he had been sentenced to death. Of the 20 remaining defendants Ribbentrop, Keitel, Kaltenbrunner, Rosenberg, Frank, Frick, Streicher, Seyss-

'IF WE CANNOT CONQUER, WE WILL DRAG THE WORLD INTO DESTRUCTION WITH US.'
Adolf Hitler

Inquart, Sauckel and Jodl were hung in the gymnasium behind the courthouse on 16 October 1946. Speer and von Schirach, the Hitler Youth leader, were sentenced to 20 years imprisonment, while Neurath received 15 years and Dönitz 10. Propaganda official Hans Fritzsche, economist Hjalmar Schacht and former vice-chancellor von Papen were acquitted of all charges. Rudolf Hess, who had been in Allied hands since his inexplicable flight to Scotland in 1941, was sent to Spandau Prison for the remainder of his life. He died there in 1986. Admiral Raeder and Walther Funk, Schacht's successor, were also sentenced to life imprisonment.

Other trials followed, some presided over by German judges.

These were less well publicized but no less shocking, not only for the enormity of the crimes that had been uncovered but for the revelations about the nature of the men who had committed them. Many of these people were so

197

unexceptional, so colourless, that it gave rise to a new phrase, 'the banality of evil'. But the public quickly tired of hearing of the horrors and the court reports grew shorter until they disappeared from the front pages. It was, perhaps, too appalling to make comfortable listening.

HITLER'S WAR

The Second World War was Hitler's war. With the invasion of Poland in September 1939 Hitler instigated the most devastating conflict in history – a conflict which raged for six long years through 27 countries and claimed the lives of an estimated 64 million people, of whom 40 million were civilians.

Six million of the victims were Jews who were systematically exterminated with chilling mechanized efficiency in concentration camps whose names are now synonymous with unimaginable suffering. Hundreds of thousands more were worked to death in slave labour camps or died of starvation and disease as a direct result of the Nazi policy of genocide.

To this toll must be added untold numbers of 'undesirables' – homosexuals, political rivals, the disabled, people privy to potentially embarrassing secrets about the Führer's past, as well as partisans and resistance fighters executed without trial and hundreds of thousands of innocent men, women and children in the occupied countries who were arbitrarily murdered in reprisals for alleged acts of resistance.

In Eastern Europe whole communities were obliterated in a day as the scourge of Hitler's death squads sated their bloodlust in scenes of savagery unseen since the Dark Ages.

And of course millions of German civilians died as a result of the fighting on the home front and in the Allied bombing raids which left their country in ruins. In the aftermath, the two superpowers, the USA and the Soviet Union, faced off across a Europe divided by barbed wire and minefields in a Cold War that threatened nuclear Armageddon for four decades to come. This was Adolf Hitler's legacy.

Auschwitz Camp Two, where at least 900,000 Jews, 75,000 Poles and 19,000 Gypsies perished

CONCLUSION

Adolf Hitler has exerted a morbid fascination for successive generations and will no doubt continue to enthrall many more, primarily because his rise and fall – and that of the nation he led – was the stuff of myth. He had little formal education, he showed little promise of 'greatness' and he possessed no artistic gifts – yet he rose to rule a cultured nation which had produced many men of intellectual and artistic genius.

With the exception of one act of bravery, for which he received the Iron Cross, he did not have an outstanding record in the First World War. In fact he was denied promotion, remaining at the lowly rank of corporal. Yet he became the supreme commander of the German armed forces and conquered most of Europe, using tactics that were often thought reckless by his own generals.

Even though he forbade his troops to retreat when common sense demanded they withdraw to fight another day, a generation of young German men still died believing implicitly in their Führer.

How can we account for this phenomenon? He was unattractive, even comical, in appearance and singularly lacking in personal charm, humour or warmth and yet he was idolized by millions – admired by German men, worshipped by German youth and adored by his female followers. An entire nation lived under his indomitable will, but they should not be seen as innocent victims. On the contrary, the German people were willing collaborators in the New Order.

Hitler appealed to their vanity and inflated sense of national pride. Crucially, he exploited their bitterness at the harsh terms imposed upon them by the Versailles Treaty, as well as voicing their inherent suspicion of the Jews who provided them with a convenient scapegoat for all their problems.

He has been portrayed as a diabolical figure who mesmerized and terrorized millions after seizing power through a combination of violence and intimidation and then betrayed the trust of the masses, but the fact is that the German people voted him into power, enthusiastically endorsed his policies and did not protest when he deprived their Jewish neighbours of their rights, their property and, finally, their lives.

Hitler had no justification for his hatred of the Jews, no personal vendetta to fulfil, yet he spewed forth his vitriol on a race who could be said to have a greater claim to German ancestry than he did, being an Austrian, an 'outsider'.

His anti-Semitism was a classic case of transference – he accused an entire race of everything he hated in himself and used them to justify his psychosis. He accused the Jews of seeking to take over the world in order to destroy it, but that is no more than a summation of his own ambitions.

He was the archetypal *untermensch* that he claimed to despise, the uneducated brute bereft of conscience or morality and tormented by his own inadequacies. He was the monster in the mirror – our primal self bereft of the soul which makes us human and which gives us hope.

> 'WHY CAN'T I CALL HITLER MY FRIEND? WHAT IS MISSING? EVERYTHING WAS MISSING. NEVER IN MY LIFE HAVE I MET A PERSON WHO SO SELDOM REVEALED HIS FEELINGS, AND IF HE DID SO, INSTANTLY LOCKED THEM AWAY AGAIN.'
> *Albert Speer*

This tragic but utterly irredeemable figure has inspired more biographies than almost any other figure in history – many more than those whose lives, ideas and deeds were much more worthy of record – for the simple but unpalatable fact that he embodied the flip side of the human personality. Hitler was not a monster or a madman but a human being utterly lacking in compassion, in humanity.

In 1942 an SS pamphlet was issued to help its members recognize the archetypal enemy of the German people, the *untermensch*, or sub-human, which it described as *'a mere projection of a man... His inmost being is a cruel chaos of wild, unbridled passions – an unbounded will to destruction, the most primitive desires, undisguised baseness... [The] Sub-human... hated the work of the other. He raged against it – secretly, as a thief; publicly as a slanderer, as a murderer. Like found like. Beast called to beast. Never did sub-human give peace. For what he needed was semi-darkness, was chaos. He shunned the light of cultural progress. What he needed for his self-preservation was the morass, was hell...'*

A more accurate portrait of Adolf Hitler would be hard to find.

Dark days for the Reich: Bormann, Goering, Hitler and Himmler stare failure in the face, 1944

TIMELINE

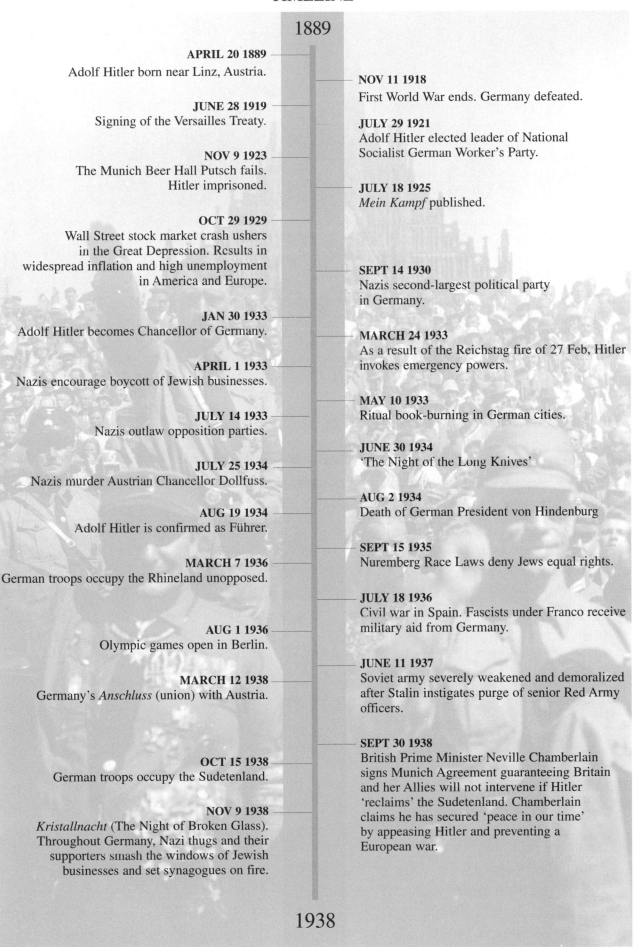

1889

APRIL 20 1889
Adolf Hitler born near Linz, Austria.

JUNE 28 1919
Signing of the Versailles Treaty.

NOV 9 1923
The Munich Beer Hall Putsch fails.
Hitler imprisoned.

OCT 29 1929
Wall Street stock market crash ushers
in the Great Depression. Results in
widespread inflation and high unemployment
in America and Europe.

JAN 30 1933
Adolf Hitler becomes Chancellor of Germany.

APRIL 1 1933
Nazis encourage boycott of Jewish businesses.

JULY 14 1933
Nazis outlaw opposition parties.

JULY 25 1934
Nazis murder Austrian Chancellor Dollfuss.

AUG 19 1934
Adolf Hitler is confirmed as Führer.

MARCH 7 1936
German troops occupy the Rhineland unopposed.

AUG 1 1936
Olympic games open in Berlin.

MARCH 12 1938
Germany's *Anschluss* (union) with Austria.

OCT 15 1938
German troops occupy the Sudetenland.

NOV 9 1938
Kristallnacht (The Night of Broken Glass).
Throughout Germany, Nazi thugs and their
supporters smash the windows of Jewish
businesses and set synagogues on fire.

NOV 11 1918
First World War ends. Germany defeated.

JULY 29 1921
Adolf Hitler elected leader of National
Socialist German Worker's Party.

JULY 18 1925
Mein Kampf published.

SEPT 14 1930
Nazis second-largest political party
in Germany.

MARCH 24 1933
As a result of the Reichstag fire of 27 Feb, Hitler
invokes emergency powers.

MAY 10 1933
Ritual book-burning in German cities.

JUNE 30 1934
'The Night of the Long Knives'

AUG 2 1934
Death of German President von Hindenburg

SEPT 15 1935
Nuremberg Race Laws deny Jews equal rights.

JULY 18 1936
Civil war in Spain. Fascists under Franco receive
military aid from Germany.

JUNE 11 1937
Soviet army severely weakened and demoralized
after Stalin instigates purge of senior Red Army
officers.

SEPT 30 1938
British Prime Minister Neville Chamberlain
signs Munich Agreement guaranteeing Britain
and her Allies will not intervene if Hitler
'reclaims' the Sudetenland. Chamberlain
claims he has secured 'peace in our time'
by appeasing Hitler and preventing a
European war.

1938

TIMELINE

1939

MARCH 15–16 1939
Nazis take Czechoslovakia.

MAY 22 1939
Nazis sign 'Pact of Steel' with Italy.

AUG 21 1939
Nazis and Soviets sign Non-aggression Pact, leaving Germany free to attack the West without fear of a second front being opened up to the east.

SEPT 3 1939
Britain, France, Australia and New Zealand declare war on Germany.

SEPT 29 1939
Nazis and Soviets divide up Poland.

NOV 8 1939
Assassination attempt on Hitler fails.

NOV 30 1939
Soviet Army invades Finland. On 12 March, Finland signs a peace treaty.

MAY 15 1940
Holland surrenders. Belgium capitulates on May 28.

MAY 26 1940
Evacuation of Allied troops from Dunkirk. Ends June 3.

JUNE 14 1940
German troops enter Paris.

JUNE 22 1940
Hitler humiliates France by forcing its leaders to sign an armistice in the same railway carriage in which Germany signed the surrender in 1918.

JULY 1 1940
German U-boat campaign begins in the Atlantic harassing merchant convoys bringing vital supplies to the British Isles.

SEPT 13 1940
Italians invade Egypt.

SEPT 15 1940
German air raids extend to Southampton, Bristol, Cardiff, Liverpool and Manchester.

OCT 7 1940
German troops invade Romania.

OCT 12 1940
Germans cancel Operation Sealion.

NOV 20 1940
Hungary joins the Axis followed three days later by Romania.

MARCH 28 1939
Spanish Civil War ends. Franco's fascists take power.

AUG 25 1939
In response Britain and Poland sign a Mutual Assistance Treaty.

SEPT 1 1939
Nazis invade Poland.

SEPT 17 1939
Soviet Army invades Poland. Ten days later, Poland surrenders.

OCTOBER 1939
Nazis instigate euthanasia policy. The sick and disabled were exterminated.

APRIL 9 1940
Nazis invade Denmark and Norway.

MAY 10 1940
Blitzkrieg! Nazis invade France, Belgium, Luxembourg and the Netherlands. Winston Churchill appointed British Prime Minister.

JUNE 10 1940
Norway surrenders; Italy declares war on Britain and France.

JUNE 16 1940
Marshal Pétain becomes French Prime Minister.

JUNE 18 1940
Hitler and Mussolini form alliance; Soviets occupy the Baltic States.

JUNE 28 1940
Britain recognizes the exiled General Charles de Gaulle as the leader of the Free French. In France the 'puppet' Vichy government collaborates with the Nazis.

JULY 10 1940
Battle of Britain begins. Throughout August, German bombers target British airfields and factories. The British respond by bombing Berlin – the first long-range raid of the war.

SEPT 27 1940
Axis formed when Germany, Italy and Japan sign the Tripartite Pact.

OCT 28 1940
Italian army invades Greece.

DEC 9–10 1940
British North African campaign begins against the Italians.

1940

TIMELINE

JAN 22 1941
British and Australians take strategically vital North African port of Tobruk which will change hands several times after Rommel's Afrika Korps enter the desert theatre on 12 Feb.

MARCH 27 1941
A coup in Yugoslavia overthrows the pro-Axis government.

APRIL 6 1941
Nazis invade Greece and Yugoslavia. The latter surrenders on 17 April. Greece surrenders ten days later.

MAY 10 1941
Deputy Führer Rudolf Hess flies to Scotland and is arrested.

MAY 27 1941
Nazi flagship, the *Bismarck*, sunk by the British Navy.

JUNE 1941
Nazi SS Einsatzgruppen begin programme of mass murder in Latvia.

JUNE 22 1941
German invasion of Soviet Union codenamed Operation Barbarossa.

JULY 3 1941
Stalin orders a scorched earth policy in the face of the advancing Germans.

JULY 12 1941
British and Soviets sign Mutual Assistance Agreement.

JULY 31 1941
Goering instructs Heydrich to instigate the Final Solution – the mass extermination of the Jews in Germany.

SEPT 1 1941
Nazis order Jews to wear yellow stars.

SEPT 3 1941
First experimental use of gas chambers at Auschwitz.

OCT 2 1941
Operation Typhoon begins (German advance on Moscow). Withdrawal begins 5 Dec. Four days later, Soviet Army launches a major counter-offensive around Moscow. German retreat begins.

DEC 7 1941
Japanese bomb Pearl Harbor.

DEC 19 1941
Hitler takes complete command of the German Army.

JAN 20 1942
SS Leader Heydrich holds the Wannsee Conference to coordinate the 'Final Solution'.

MAY 30 1942
First thousand-bomber British air raid (against Cologne).

JUNE 1942
Mass murder of Jews begins at Auschwitz.

JUNE 4 1942
Heydrich dies after assassination attempt in Prague. Nazis liquidate Lidice in reprisal.

JUNE 11 1942
Himmler orders the destruction of Jewish ghettos in Poland.

JULY 1–30 1942
First Battle of El Alamein.

SEPT 1942
Battle of Stalingrad begins.

JAN 14–24 1943
At Casablanca, Churchill and Roosevelt demand the unconditional surrender of Germany.

JAN 27 1943
First American bombing raid on Germany.

FEB 2 1943
Encircled Germans surrender at Stalingrad.

FEB 18 1943
Nazis arrest White Rose resistance leaders in Munich.

APRIL 19 1943
Waffen SS launch assault on Jewish resistance group in the Warsaw ghetto. Resistance holds out until 16 May.

MAY 13 1943
German and Italian troops surrender in North Africa.

JULY 9–10 1943
Allies land in Sicily.

JULY 25–26 1943
Mussolini arrested and replaced by Marshal Badoglio. He is rescued six weeks later by the Germans.

OCT 1 1943
Allies enter Naples, Italy.

1943

TIMELINE

1944

JAN 22 1944
Allies land at Anzio.

FEB 15–18 1944
Allies bomb the monastery of Monte Cassino.

JUNE 5 1944
Allies enter Rome.

JUNE 6 1944
D-Day landings.

JUNE 22 1944
The Soviet summer offensive begins the rout of the German invaders.

JULY 20 1944
Hitler survives assassination attempt at the 'Wolf's Lair' HQ.

AUG 25 1944
Paris liberated.

SEPT 17 1944
Operation Market Garden begins (Allied airborne assault on Holland).

OCT 14 1944
Allies liberate Athens; Rommel commits suicide on Hitler's orders for his part in the July plot.

DEC 26 1944
The 'Battling Bastards of Bastogne' relieved by General Patton. The Germans withdraw from the Ardennes during January. Hitler's last gamble has failed.

FEB 13–14 1945
Dresden is destroyed by a firestorm after Allied bombing raids.

APRIL 1 1945
US troops encircle remnants of German army in the Ruhr. They surrender on 18 April.

APRIL 16 1945
Americans enter Nuremberg.

APRIL 21 1945
Soviets enter Berlin.

APRIL 29 1945
US 7th Army liberates Dachau.

MAY 7 1945
The unconditional surrender of the German forces is signed.

MAY 9 1945
Hermann Goering surrenders to US 7th Army.

JUNE 5 1945
Allies partition Germany and divide Berlin into sections. The Cold War begins.

JAN 27 1944
The siege of Leningrad is lifted after 900 days.

MARCH 4 1944
First major daylight bombing raid on Berlin by the Allies.

JUNE 13 1944
First German V1 rocket attack on Britain.

JULY 3 1944
'Battle of the Hedgerows' in Normandy. A week later, Caen is liberated.

JULY 24 1944
Soviet troops liberate first concentration camp at Majdanek.

SEPT 13 1944
US troops reach the Siegfried Line.

OCT 2 1944
Polish Home Army forced to surrender to the Germans in Warsaw after weeks of heroic resistance.

DEC 16–27 1944
Battle of the Bulge in the Ardennes. Retreating Waffen SS murder 81 US POWs at Malmedy.

JAN 26 1945
Soviet troops liberate Auschwitz.

FEB 4–11 1945
Roosevelt, Churchill, Stalin meet at Yalta and plan the partition of post-war Germany.

APRIL 1945
Allies recover stolen Nazi art hidden in salt mines.

APRIL 12 1945
Allies uncover the horrors of the 'Final Solution' at Buchenwald and Belsen concentration camps; President Roosevelt dies. Truman becomes President.

APRIL 28 1945
Mussolini is hanged by Italian partisans.

APRIL 30 1945
Adolf Hitler commits suicide in the Berlin bunker, followed by the suicide of Goebbels. The corpses are burnt.

MAY 8 1945
VE (Victory in Europe) Day.

MAY 23 1945
SS Reichsführer Himmler commits suicide.

NOV 20 1945
Nuremberg war crimes trials begin. Goering will commit suicide almost a year later, two hours before his scheduled execution.

1945

REFERENCES:

Bloch, Dr, *in The Psychoanalytic Quarterly*, 1947

Das kleine ABC des Nationalsozialisten, Nazi Party pamphlet, 1922

Das Reich, November 1941

Deutsche Wehr, official German army magazine, 1925

Die Vollmacht des Gewissens (Munich 1956)

Dietrich, Otto, *12 Years With Hitler* (Munich 1955)

Fest, Joachim, *Hitler: A Biography*, (Harcourt 1973)

Flaherty, Thomas, *Centre of the Web* (Time Life 2004)

Frank, Hans, *Im Angesicht des Galgens* (Alfred Beck 1953)

Goering, *Aufbau einer Nation*, 1934

Halder, General, Chief of the Army General Staff, Diary of

Heiden, Konrad, *Der Führer* (Houghton-Mifflin 1944)

Hitler, Adolf, *Mein Kampf* (Boston 1943)

Hoover Institute, Abel file

IMT document, 1919-PS, XXIX

Jetzinger, Franz, *Hitler's Youth* (Hutchinson, London 1958)

Kleist, Peter, *The European Tragedy*, (Times Press 1965)

Kohler, Pauline OSS sourcebook 1936

Krüger, Horst, *A Crack In The Wall* (Fromm International 1966)

Kubizek, August, *The Young Hitler I Knew* (Boston 1955)

Langer, Walter, OSS sourcebook 1936,

Lloyd-George, David, *Daily Express*, 'I Talked To Hitler', 17 November 1936

Ludecke, Kurt, *I Knew Hitler*, 1938

Moltke, Helmuth James von, *Letzte Briefe aus dem Gefängnis Tegel* (Berlin 1963)

Musmanno, Michael, *Ten Days To Die* (New York 1950)

Neuhäusler, *Kreuz and Hakenkreuz* (Munich 1946)

OSS sourcebook 1943

Pechel, Rudolf, *Deutscher Widerstand* (Erlenbach-Zurich 1947)

Rauschning, *The Voice of Destruction* (New York 1940)

Remak, Joachim, *The Nazi Years* (Prentice Hall, NJ 1969)

Shirer, William L, *The Rise and Fall of the Third Reich* (Mandarin 1991)

Sognnaes & Strom, 'The Odontological Identification of Adolf Hitler: Definitive Documentation By X-Rays, Interrogations and Autopsy Findings', 1973 *Acta Odontologica Scandinavica* 31

Speer, Albert, *Inside The Third Reich* (Bonanza, New York 1982)

Strasser, Otto, *The Gangsters Around Hitler* (London 1942)

Vierteljahreshefte fur Zeitgeschichte, VI

Völkischer Beobachter, 1921

Völkischer Beobachter, 3 March 1932

Waite, Robert G L, *The Psychopathic God* (Basic Books 1977)

ACKNOWLEDGMENTS:

The author wishes to acknowledge the following as primary sources of background information and quotations:

Flaherty, Thomas, *Centre of the Web* (Time Life 2004)

Remak, Joachim, *The Nazi Years* (Prentice Hall, NJ 1969)

Shirer, William L, *The Rise and Fall of the Third Reich* (Mandarin 1991)

Speer, Albert, *Inside The Third Reich* (Bonanza, New York 1982)

Waite, Robert GL, *The Psychopathic God* (Basic Books 1977)

SOURCES & NOTES: (See also References above.)

1 (Page 12) *Hitler: A Biography*, Joachim Fest

2 (16) Walter Langer, US Office of Strategic Studies Report

3 (16) *Im Angesicht des Galgens*, Dr Hans Frank

4 (22) 'The Odontological Identification of Adolf Hitler: Definitive Documentation By X-Rays, Interrogations and Autopsy Findings', Sognnaes and Strom

Note: Hitler's monorchidism was discovered during a Soviet autopsy on the Führer's charred remains conducted in 1945. Although the identity of the body found in the grounds of the Reich chancellory has been disputed, it was subsequently formally identified as being that of Hitler by an independent team of Norwegian and American dental experts.

5 (23) Interview with Pauline Kohler, US OSS sourcebook

6 (26) *The Psychoanalytic Quarterly*

7 (35) *Ten Days To Die*, Michael Musmanno

8 (39) *The Voice of Destruction*, Hermann Rauschning

9 (44) *Mein Kampf*

10 (45) **Note**: Edward Grey (1862–1933) was a British statesman

11 (52) The programme was drawn largely from Hitler's speech that day, 24 February 1920

12 (59) *Völkischer Beobachter* 1921

13 (59) *Der Führer*, Konrad Heiden

14 (60) Nazi party pamphlet *Das kleine abc des Nationalsozialisten*

15 (70) *The Gangsters Around Hitler*, Otto Strasser

16 (78) *Völkischer Beobachter* 3 March 1932

17 (84) Ernst Röhm to Kurt Ludecke June 1933 (quoted in Ludecke's *I Knew Hitler*)

18 (98) US OSS sourcebook 1943

19 (98) 'I Talked To Hitler', *The Daily Express*

20 (102) *The European Tragedy*, Kleist

21 (104) *Aufbau einer Nation*, Hermann Goering

22 (108) Hitler in informal conversation, 22 February 1942

23 (115) *Kreuz and Hakenkreuz*, Johannes Neuhäusler

24 (118) *Emmi Bonhoeffer: Essay, Gespräch, Erinnerung*, 2004

25 (121) *Das Reich*, November 1941

26 (121) IMT document 1919-PS, XXIX

27 (125) Abel file, Hoover Institute

28 (136) *Vierteljahreshefte fur Zeitgeschichte*

29 (136) *12 Years With Hitler*, Otto Dietrich

30 (146) *Die Vollmacht des Gewissens*

31 (161) Extract from the diary of Hans Frank

32 (190) *Letzte Briefe aus dem Gefängnis Tegel*, Helmuth James Graf von Moltke, Berlin 1945

33 (191) *Deutscher Widerstand*, Rudolf Pechel

PICTURE CREDITS